MY FAVOURITE PRAYERS

Written by: Janice Price
Design by: Kelly Nicholls
Edited by: Barbara Walters-Ennis

Printed on recyclable products (ie paper)
Printed in China

CONTENTS

MORNING PRAYERS

MORNING PRAYERS

Dear Lord,

You are a beautiful Father.

I pray that You help me to be brave today.

Fill me up and take over.

I cannot go through this day on my own.

I need You with me, and Your angels completely around me.

Every step I take today, I pray You be in my heart.

I pray You please hold up my feet with Your strong hands.

This day ahead may be hard, but nothing shall put me down because I am lifted by You.

I cannot go over this day and I cannot go under it, but with You I will go through this day You have made.

Thank You for getting me through this day.

I love You.

In the name of Jesus, Amen.

Dear Lord,

I trust in You for a great day today.

I will walk in love wherever I go today.

I will be kind and friendly to others,

I will be cheerful to those who are upset and I will share what I have with other people.

I pray I will have the strength to walk in the love You have given me Lord so that no matter what happens I will walk in love.

I will be bold in love.

I will not let anything stop me, because love overcomes all things.

Thank You for Your love, I love You.

In the name of Jesus, Amen.

Dear Lord,

You are so kind to me.

I pray that today I will get done all that I need to do.

Nothing will stop me today.

I pray I will finish every little thing that I plan to do.

Nothing is too small that I can forget, because I am small and You never forget me.

I will finish every big thing that I plan to do.

Nothing is too big for me because You are with me Lord.

I will be very quick when I need to be fast and very slow when I need to be quiet.

You always listen to me when I want to speak to You, so I will do very good listening today and follow instructions.

Thank You Lord, I love You.

In the name of Jesus, Amen.

Dear Lord,

You are happiness and You are brightness.

I didn't wake up happy today but I will find my happiness in You.

I will be happy at how You love me, happy at how You listen to me, happy at how You look after me, happy at how You keep me safe.

I will be happy today so that I can make other people happy, like how You make me happy.

You are my joy and I find my joy in You.

You are my delight and I find my delight in You.

You are my excitement and I find my excitement in You.

Because You are in me, I find joy and delight and excitement in me.

I dance and sing because of You.

Thank You for my happiness, I love You.

In the name of Jesus, Amen.

Dear Lord,

I love You and thank You because You have been so kind to give me another day and another opportunity.

Today is the day You have made!

Today I will praise You, because You are such a loving sweet Father, and You are perfect in every single way.

Today will be the day that I face my fears, because You live in me, and give me the courage to do all things.

Today is the day that I walk in love because You are love, and You complete me.

I will speak sweet words and be extra kind.

Today is the day You have made for me.

And I will use every moment You give me to get close to You, because there is nothing I want more.

I pray You help me to be closer to You each day and to continue to love You more each day.

In the name of Jesus, Amen.

Dear Lord

Thank You for the present day that I have.

Today is called the present because it is a present from You.

I must cherish each day and not live in the past but in the present.

I thank You that the old has gone and I am now here.

I will not stay in the past but I will live each moment that You give to me.

Anything that was sad yesterday will not be sad today because I have again been washed by Your joy Lord.

Thank You for a new day and a new opportunity.

I love You.

In the name of Jesus, Amen.

Dear Lord

Thank You for my energy today.

I am fresh in Your presence.

I am awake and full of life.

I am excited for such a great day ahead and I am ready with all of my energy.

I am joyful and jolly.

There is no tiredness in me, thank You Father.

I feel as fresh as if a bucket of water fell on me.

I feel as rested as if I have been sleeping for hours and hours and hours.

I am restored because You give me the energy.

Thank You Lord, I love You.

In the name of Jesus, Amen.

Dear Lord

My eyes are open and I am ready to see You in my day today.

My ears are open and I am ready to hear You in my day today.

My heart is open and I am ready to feel You in my day today.

I want an experience with You Father today.

I want to be surrounded by You Lord today.

It is all my heart wants.

I am seeking after You today and I will find You.

Thank You Lord for Your presence, thank You Lord for this day.

I love You.

In the name of Jesus, Amen.

Dear Lord

I cannot live this day without You.

I need You Father to completely take control of this day.

Father, I need You to rain Your love on me and fill me up until I overflow.

I pray that I see You everywhere that I look today.

Father this day is Yours and I give it all to You.

Father, today, everything that I do is for You.

Today I live as Your child, and everything You make me.

I am Your miracle.

Father, thank You.

This is a beautiful day thank You.

I will give You all praise today because You deserve it all.

I trust You, I put this day in Your hands, and it is Yours.

Thank You.

In the name of Jesus, Amen.

Dear Lord

You are so wonderful.

I pray for You to be my shelter today.

Watch over me as I walk through this day.

Everything that tries to stop me will not affect me, because no matter how big it is or strong it is, You are my shelter.

You are stronger than all things and so You will not let anything pass through Your cover to touch me.

You are like a strong big house when it is raining.

No matter how heavy it rains or how strong it rains, no rain can touch me.

Thank You Father.

Only if I step out of Your shelter can something touch me.

So I keep safe in You today, thank You.

I love You.

In the name of Jesus, Amen.

BEDTIME PRAYERS

Dear Lord

I love You.

I pray You bless me as I sleep, and pray You keep me safe and warm.

I pray and thank You, because Your angels surround me.

They give me a sweet sleep and I am guarded and protected at all times.

Thank You Father.

I pray that I do not have any scary dreams that make me scared as I sleep.

I do not need to fear because You are here at all times, even when I am sleeping.

You watch over me and You protect me.

I pray for peace as I sleep, peace knowing that I do not have to worry.

Peace as a child of God, knowing I am being watched at all times.

Thank You, I love You.

In the name of Jesus I pray, Amen.

Dear Lord

Your presence is so sweet to me.

I pray that You visit me as I sleep.

I pray that I see You and You reveal Yourself to me as I dream.

I pray that I dream of You and about You.

I pray that my dreams are filled with You.

I pray that Your presence washes over me and through me, like a lovely ocean, as I sleep.

I pray that if I awake at any time You reveal to me Your beautiful voice.

And I pray that I feel the warm presence of the Holy Spirit.

I love You.

In the name of Jesus I pray, Amen.

Dear Lord

I pray for Your mighty presence to rush through me as I sleep.

I pray for a gentle and comforting sleep.

I pray for a restful and undisturbed sleep.

Thank You for giving me a sweet and peaceful sleep.

Father, I pray that You restore each of my brain cells as I take my sleep and You build me up.

I pray You fill me up with Your love as I sleep.

I pray for a good sleep so I do not feel tired or down.

I pray for an easy sleep tonight, and all nights.

Be with me as I sleep and cover me with Your gentle presence, restoring me completely.

Thank You, I trust You and I love You.

In the name of Jesus I pray, Amen

Dear Lord

Thank You for this day that I have had.

I love You so much and I thank You, that You were with me every moment and every step of my day.

No matter what happened today, I will go to sleep knowing that You are with me and You never leave me.

I go to sleep tonight happy because it is another day I have had breath.

I go to sleep in love because I know that You love me so much.

You have chosen me, I am Your child and I am Your treasure.

Thank You for this day, and I pray You give me sweet dreams.

In the name of Jesus I pray, Amen.

Dear Lord

There is nothing more beautiful than You.

I pray that You speak to me in my sleep tonight.

I pray for an experience with You, and I pray You answer my prayers in my sleep.

As I dream of beautiful things tonight, show me the direction I should take.

As I dream of wonderful things tonight, guide my decisions.

I pray for the answers, and trust You to deliver tonight or in Your own chosen time.

I am open and aware to You.

Thank You, I trust You and I love You.

In the name of Jesus I pray, Amen.

Dear Lord

You are the most perfect.

As I am now going to sleep, I pray for Your peace to rush through me.

I pray for a peaceful sleep, I pray for a sweet gentle sleep.

I pray that my sleep is not interrupted unless it is by You and for a reason.

Thank You Father.

I pray that as I sleep I feel warm, wrapped up in Your arms, and that every loud sound is hidden from me with Your hands.

I pray for complete peace as I sleep, and I thank You for it.

I love You.

In the name of Jesus I pray, Amen.

Dear Lord

I praise Your precious name.

I pray You bless me.

I pray for sweet dreams.

Help me to get to sleep tonight.

Father, even though there are so many things around me and so many things on my mind, I pray for quiet and to be calm.

Father, I pray You clear my mind so I can focus on You alone.

I pray that only You are on my thoughts as I go to sleep.

I trust You, and I am leaving all of my thoughts with You because I believe You know better, You are powerful enough to do anything, and You love me.

I love You and I pray to see You as I sleep, it would be beautiful. In the name of Jesus I pray, Amen.

Dear Lord

Thank You for the day that You have given me today.

Thank You for each breath and each moment.

No one else gives breath in my lungs, and I thank You.

I pray for another day tomorrow.

I pray that I dream of You as I sleep.

I pray that You guide me in my sleep, and when I wake up that I remember what You said to me.

I love You, and I will never stop.

Good night Father.

I pray for all of those who go to sleep tonight, that they have lovely dreams, and they hear You.

I pray for all of those going to sleep, that they are protected by Your strong arms; You are stronger than all things.

I love You.

I trust You with my prayers, and I believe in You.

In the name of Jesus I pray, Amen.

Dear Lord

Thank You for another day.

I am excited for the day tomorrow.

I pray that Your plans be done, that my plans are Your plans for me.

Thank You for the sleep I am now taking.

I am excited for an exciting day tomorrow.

No matter what it looks like or I feel like, I am excited for tomorrow because You are in complete control.

I am excited for tomorrow because it is another day with You, You have so much in store for me.

Tomorrow will be such an adventure and I can't wait to be in Your presence.

Give me sweet dreams, I pray.

Thank You for each day, another opportunity to spend with You and be closer to You, and to be more like Jesus.

I love You my Father.

Goodnight.

In the name of Jesus I pray, Amen.

Dear Lord

Thank You for my bedtime.

It has been a long busy day and I am so thankful I am able to snuggle into bed right now.

Make everything around me feel soft and comfy on my skin.

I pray that I fall asleep as soon as my head hits the pillow.

It has been very tiring today and I thank You that I am able to go to sleep now.

Thank You Father for this beautiful sleeping place.

I pray You cover where I sleep with Your presence, so I can see You and feel You, when I wake up.

I love You.

In the name of Jesus I pray, Amen.

PRAYERS OF THANKSGIVING

Dear Lord

Thank You for every breath.

Thank You for the life I have and the gift to get this far.

Each breath is a reminder of Your presence, and nothing shall hurt me.

Thank You Father for each heartbeat, that I live another second.

Thank You Father for each blink of my eyes I have experienced, I have lost count of the amount of times You have provided me to blink.

Every second is precious and I thank You Lord that You have given me more than a million seconds!

I will make every second be worthy, I will value every second as it is so precious.

No matter what happens I thank You that I have breath, and You are in each of my heartbeats.

I love You and I am so thankful.

In the name of Jesus I pray, Amen.

Dear Lord

Thank You for choosing me.

Thank You for choosing me to be Your child.

There is no other like You.

You love me so much, thank You.

You treasure me so much, thank You.

I have been chosen to be a child of God, how precious.

Thank You for wanting a relationship with me, and thank You for wanting me to be close to You.

Because I really want to be close to You, at all times, thank You.

Words are not enough but I must live a life of thankfulness.

At all times I will thank You.

Thank You for everything it means to be Your child.

Thank You that You created me for a reason and for a purpose.

I love You always.

In the name of Jesus I pray, Amen.

Dear Lord

Thank You for who You are, and everything You are.

There is none like You.

None as powerful or loving, and I thank You that I can call on You at all times.

You never lie and You never let me down, I trust You at all times in all things, thank You.

I thank You that I can call out to You as my Father, and You answer me always.

Thank You that You are not only God to me, thank You that You are not only Lord to me, but thank You that I can call You dad, daddy and father.

There is no other more worthy than You, thank You I can call You my Father.

I love You.

In the name of Jesus I pray, Amen.

Dear Lord

Thank You for who I am because of You.

Thank You for filling me with life and happiness.

Thank You that no matter what happens I will have peace because I know You are right here in me.

Thank You that I am bold and brave because You live inside me and I can do all things as a child of God.

Thank You that I have complete peace because I can give You all my worries and trust You are able and mighty to sort it all out for me.

Thank You for my purpose that I have a reason for being here and by You I am able to achieve.

Thank You that I have a heart filled with love because of You, I am able to overcome hate with love.

Thank You, I love You.

In the name of Jesus I pray, Amen.

Dear Lord

Thank You for all of the special people in my life.

Thank You that I see You Lord when I look at them.

Thank You for shining through them and showing me Your presence.

Thank for how loving and caring people are to me.

Thank You for each memory that I share with my loved ones, thank You for each precious moment.

Thank You Father that I have people who love me and care for me.

Thank You that I have people who help me and look after me.

Lord I will show my gratefulness by treating my loved ones as they are very valuable.

Each person in my life is a gift by You, and so I must treasure my gifts.

Thank You Father that I have people to talk to and have fun with. I love You.

In the name of Jesus I pray, Amen.

Dear Lord

Thank You for the doors of success You open wide for me.

Thank You that I have favour with all people, because I am a child of God and all will see the light that You are shining in me.

Thank You that I will get rewarded for things because I am Your child.

Thank You that my whole life will be successful because we go through everything together and grow through everything together.

Thank You Lord that there is something special about me that is You in me.

Thank for all the times I was told yes when other people thought it would be a no.

Thank You for all the things that seem impossible are made possible through You.

I love You.

In the name of Jesus I pray, Amen.

Dear Lord

Thank You for the safety You provide me.

I know that as Your child I am protected from all things, and nothing shall harm me.

I am protected by Your presence and Your strong shelter.

Thank You, that because of You I have protection stronger than anything else.

Thank You that Your protection is strong enough to protect me from the biggest things and the smallest things.

Thank You that I do not have to worry because You are here.

Thank You that You watch out for me when I do not or when I cannot, You are better than all others.

Thank You that I am happy and safe in Your arms.

I love You.

In the name of Jesus I pray, Amen.

Dear Lord

Thank You for all I have.

Thank You for everything that You have gifted me with.

I am so blessed to have all that I have.

Even if I feel I do not have what someone else has, I thank You Father, because millions of people do not have what I have.

My happiness does not depend on what things I have, because I have You, and I always will. Thank You for the gift of You.

Each and everything that I own I will say thank You for.

I will not think about what I do not have, but I will thank You for everything that I do have.

The amount of things that You have given me will take forever and ever to count.

You are such a loving providing God.

Thank You and I love You.

In the name of Jesus I pray, Amen.

Dear Lord

I love You very much.

Thank You sweet Father for every second of breath.

Thank You Father, for each moment You give me to spend with You.

Thank You for each new day; it is such a special gift, the present.

Thank You for each opportunity You provide me to do something I did not get to do yesterday.

Thank You Father that You fill me up completely with boldness and confidence, so I have the courage to do things I could not do yesterday.

Thank You Father, because You open doors to new opportunities I would not have without You.

You are so lovely and I thank You.

In the name of Jesus I pray, Amen.

Dear Lord

Thank You for Your precious Son Jesus and the sweet Holy Spirit.

Father, You give me all I need.

I am so thankful You have been so kind to me.

Thank You for providing me company in the Holy Spirit that I cannot find anywhere else.

Thank You for the guidance of the Holy Spirit.

Thank You Father for the precious gift of Jesus, who gave His life for us.

There is nothing more beautiful, that You gave Your only Son so that I can speak to You and listen to You and spend time with You.

Only You are so loving to provide like You do.

You care for me more than anyone else does or can.

I love You.

In the name of Jesus I pray, Amen.

PRAYERS FOR FAMILY

Dear Lord

I thank You my Father for my family.

I thank You for the joy that my family brings to my life and the lives of others each and every day.

I thank You for granting them Courage when they feel afraid.

Happiness when they feel sad.

Confidence where they have doubts.

Laughter when they want to cry.

The ability to Smile when their spirit is low.

Patience to let Thy will be done and not theirs.

I thank You for the Sunshine to brighten up their days.

But most of all I thank You for their Faith to believe in You no matter what trials they face.

In the name of Jesus I pray, Amen.

Dear Lord

I lift up my family to You and ask that You Bless and protect them always.

I pray that You are there for them at all times, through the good times and the bad times.

I pray that when You speak to each and every one of them they hear Your words loud and clear and listen to You.

I pray that You will continue to be an encouragement to them to walk in Your ways and to follow Your guidance.

I pray that their faithfulness will grow and grow and that they will continue to glorify Your name and the name of Your precious son Jesus Christ our Lord and Saviour.

I pray that they will submit their plans to You and know that through You all things are possible.

In the name of Jesus I pray, Amen.

Dear Lord

I thank You for Your everlasting Love, Grace and forgiveness that You give to me and my family.

I thank You for our health, our strength and our prosperity and I thank You for Blessing us with peace, laughter and happiness when we are together.

I am so grateful that we come together in our faith to Praise Your name and I pray that we will continue give You thanks for all that You do in our lives.

Lord we know that You are a Mighty God and a Loving God and I pray that we will take care of each other in the way that You have taken care of us as individuals and as a family.

In the name of Jesus I pray, Amen.

Dear Lord

I place my family in Your loving arms, and I ask that You take care of them as we are all Your children and You are our Father.

Lord help us to learn from our mistakes and walk in Your footsteps.

Teach us to trust you completely and grant us the discipline to show compassion even when we are angry and to show love despite feeling fear and frustration.

Help us to use Your mercy and grace to build our character.

Allow us to always be mindful of Your presence and rest in the knowledge that we are deeply loved by You.

In the name of Jesus I pray, Amen.

Dear Lord

I thank You for my parents.

I thank You for making them to be kind, loving and caring parents.

I thank You for granting my parents the knowledge and the patience to understand me.

To know that no matter what I love them so much that I would not know what to do without them.

I thank You for making my parents be a living example of how to love You as my parents are good people who lead by example.

I thank You for letting my parents raise me in their Christian faith and raise me to be a child of God so that I can grow to love You more and more each day.

In the name of Jesus I pray, Amen.

Dear Lord

My Father only You could Bless me with the family that I have.

You have given wonderful parents, beautiful grandparents and loving siblings.

I thank You for granting me the certainty that I am not only protected spiritually in my faith, but that I also have people in my life that will watch over me and take care of me whilst I am living on earth.

Lord You know what I need and You have provided this for me in my family and I am so happy because of You.

You have taught me to respect my parents, and my grandparents in the same way that I respect You and I will always remember this.

In the name of Jesus I pray, Amen.

Dear Lord

I awake each morning and I am filled with joy, laughter and happiness because I know that I am loved not only by You, but also by my family.

I know that I am loved by my mum because her eyes shine bright whenever she sees me and I know that I am loved by my dad, because his smiles always warm my heart.

I feel safe and secure whenever they are around and I know that if they are not around, I can always rely on You.

I thank You for filling me with the knowledge and courage to live in my faith, knowing that I will always be loved and protected.

In the name of Jesus I pray, Amen.

Dear Lord

I pray today for my brothers and my sisters.

I pray for our similarities and I pray for our differences.

I pray that You keep us together in our faith and show us that You placed us in the same family for a reason, as together we will always be a force to be reckoned with.

I pray that You give us the Grace to forgive and the strength to face and overcome any difficulties.

I pray that as we grow older we do not grow apart and that our love for each other is steadfast in the same way that our love for You will always stay strong.

I pray that as our age increases so too does our faith and trust in You increase.

I pray that we continue to value Your love and the love of each other.

In the name of Jesus I pray, Amen.

Dear Lord

Thank You for my family.

I know that not everyone is Blessed with a loving and wonderful family and I ask that You show Your love to those who are alone and do not have parents or grandparents to love and care for them.

I pray that You reveal Yourself to them so that Your Grace can be at work in their hearts and soul and keep them happy when their trials try to pull them apart.

I pray that Your love is enough to keep them safe and to allow them to honour and praise Your name for all the goodness that You bring into their lives.

I pray that You develop their character to show gratitude and appreciation for having You in their life, because through You nothing is impossible.

In the name of Jesus I pray, Amen.

Dear Lord

You are my Father, My Mother and My family and I will always be grateful for You for being in my life.

I thank You for the pleasure of knowing You and the Grace to feel safe in the comfort of Your love in the absence of my human family.

I will put my trust in You in the knowledge that You are my Lord and my Protector and I will take every opportunity to glorify Your name.

Lord I know that Your gifts are many and I thank You for Your wonderful Blessings that You give to me.

I thank You for continuing to make me feel special as if I am Your favourite child.

In the name of Jesus I pray, Amen.

PRAYERS FOR COURAGE

Dear Lord

Please hear my prayer.

I pray for courage on my first day.

Father You live in me and I pray that You light up in me, so that as I face my first day I know You are here with me.

You never leave me, and thank You for always being here in me, in my heart.

I have nothing to fear because You light bright in me.

I pray for favour with God and favour with people.

I pray that people will see You, the bright light shining within me.

I give every worry I have to You Father, and I believe You will be in control of it all.

I set my focus on You on my first day, and nothing else shall distract me.

Thank You for this opportunity to have a first day, I give You all the glory.

I trust that You have prepared me for what You have prepared for me.

I love You Lord.

In the name of Jesus I pray, Amen.

Dear Lord

I am praying to be brave.

Father I need Your strength; I depend on You for my strength.

Please Father provide Your strength in me that I am able to be brave to overcome my fear.

Your love what is in me overcomes all things.

Because You live in me I know that nothing shall hurt me, and that I am able to do all things, even things I am very frightened of.

Nothing will go wrong, and everything happens for a reason.

My fears are gone away and I stay in Your strength and Your safety.

I will not be held back by my fears.

Because You live in me, I am able to overcome my fears, with peace that You are here at all times.

Thank You Father for making me brave.

I love You.

In the name of Jesus I pray, Amen.

Dear Lord

I pray for wisdom for my test.

I pray You remove all fear and worry.

I pray that You remain bright in my heart so that I feel Your presence as I sit in the exam hall.

Father God I pray that every bit of knowledge and wisdom is mine.

I pray that the test paper is in my favour, every question that I see will be every question that I have studied.

I pray that in the test, the answers will be clear in my mind.

Please Father remove all distractions, nothing shall come against my success.

Father I pray for favour when the examiner is marking my test paper, I pray that my exam paper lights up in their eyes and You fill them with kindness.

Thank You Father for my success.

I will trust in You and I leave the test paper in Your hands, please Father remove all worry from me.

I love You.

In the name of Jesus I pray, Amen.

Dear Lord

Hear my prayer.

I need You as I enter this competition. I pray You remove all fear and worry as I enter.

Father I have prepared for this opportunity that You have provided.

Thank You for this opportunity, shine through me so others know that it is all You.

Father I pray that my performance is perfected in the eyes of the judges, that they see my performance as light.

I pray that there is favour upon me.

I pray that I light up in the judge's mind, that they cannot forget my performance.

I pray that they see something special in me, that I am a child of God, and that special thing is You.

I thank You Father for success, I love You.

In the name of Jesus I pray, Amen.

Dear Lord

I pray for boldness.

I pray for Your presence to take over me when I speak about You.

Father God I pray that I have boldness to speak up about something that is wrong, and boldness to speak up for those who cannot speak.

I ask that You give me the boldness to form the words that other people are not able to form, and even the words that I am not able to form.

Father I pray that You speak through me for Your glory.

Shine bright through me and in me.

I need Your light and I want Your light.

Make me bold and to help the people, by Your power alone.

Thank You for Your boldness.

Because You are in me, I am bold!

I love You.

In the name of Jesus I pray, Amen.

Dear Lord

I need You.

I have to speak boldly in front of people, and I cannot do it by myself.

I am coming to You for help Father, and thank You for being so happy to help me.

I pray for confidence and a clear voice as I speak, that nothing will stop people from hearing what I have to say.

I pray to speak with boldness and courage in front of everyone because You are with me.

Father, enter me and transform me to be filled with courage and confidence.

Thank You for Your presence, I cannot do it by myself.

I love You completely and I love that I can come to You at all times.

I have nothing to fear because nothing will go wrong, I trust You Father.

I believe You will help me speak in front of everyone.

In the name of Jesus I pray, Amen.

PRAYERS FOR COURAGE

Dear Lord

I pray for courage.

I come with my heart completely open Lord.

I have fears that are in me, but I am asking You Father to get rid of them.

I have nothing to fear because You are in me, You are with me, and You are all around me.

All of Your angels surround me, thank You.

Your strong arms protect me from all of my fears.

I pray for courage, that You will help me to stop fearing.

Thank You, because You are always there for me to go to.

Thank You because You have already, so many times, shown me that I do not need to fear.

I will not fear because I trust You Lord, I trust that You are right here, and You will not let anything that should not be, happen to me.

I believe that You are God over all things, and will do all what is best for me.

I love You.

In the name of Jesus I pray, Amen.

Dear Lord

I pray for Your help.

I am doing something for the first time and I need Your help and Your guidance and Your strength.

I cannot do it by myself, but I trust in You to help me.

I pray that You fill me up with Your presence and courage, and enter my heart.

I thank You that I do not have anything to fear because even though it is the first time, nothing will go wrong.

Nothing can go out of Your plan when You are here and have control of my life.

You tell me to have no fear, but have faith, and so I open up and let You completely remove all fear, and replace it with faith.

I have faith nothing will go wrong because I believe in You.

Yes it may be scary because I have never done it before, but after I do it the first time,

I will walk in even more boldness.

Thank You.

Thank You for holding up my steps in faith.

I love You.

In the name of Jesus I pray, Amen.

Dear Lord

Thank You for the brave person You make me.

Without You I cannot do anything, with You I can do everything.

You are a Father of power, and the same power You have given to me, because I am Your child.

The power to speak to people I would not normally be able to speak to.

The power to speak in front of huge crowds.

You give me the power to go places I would not normally be able to go to because I was not brave enough.

You have put in me power to do all things through You.

Thank You for the spirit of power You have given me.

You did not create me to live in fear, but to have faith in You at all times.

I trust You, and I love You.

I pray for the power to be brave.

In the name of Jesus I pray, Amen.

Dear Lord

Fill me up with You.

Fill me up until You pour out.

I pray I am so filled with You that You pour out to other people.

I pray that You fill my life up so much that people see You when they look at me.

When I am filled with You I cannot fear because You are completely in control.

I trust You with everything because You are amazing; there is no one else like You.

Nothing comes close to who You are.

I pray You remove any part of doubt in me that does not trust You, and replace it with Your presence.

Where You are here fear cannot remain.

You overcome all fear.

Where Your presence is, fear has to run.

I pray for Your presence every second of my life, I love You.

In the name of Jesus I pray, Amen.

PRAYERS FOR GUIDANCE

Dear Lord

Thank You for You.

Thank You for Your direction, that when I follow You I know I am on the right path, the path of righteousness.

Father I pray that I am able to stay on the path to You at all times.

Father I pray that nothing blocks my path of righteousness.

I pray if anything blocks the path that You remove it, nothing is big enough to block me.

I pray that no distractions will lead me to walk off the path of righteousness onto another path, but that You are my focus to keep straight on the path to You.

Help me to only see You ahead of me.

In Jesus name I pray, Amen

PRAYERS FOR GUIDANCE

Dear Lord

I pray that You show me clearly Your guidance for me.

Father I pray that You speak to me about what to do and where to go to follow You on the path of righteousness.

I pray that You reveal Yourself to me so that I see and encounter and experience Your direction onto the path of righteousness.

Father I pray that You make it very clear to me what Your guidance is, so that I do not get confused by other guidance.

I pray I make no mistakes and I see You.

Thank You, I love You.

In the name of Jesus I pray, Amen.

Dear Lord

I thank You for Your wisdom.

Oh powerful mighty God, You are yesterday today and tomorrow.

You know all things and all things concerning my future.

Because I trust in You I shall place my future into Your hands Lord.

I let You take control and the lead over my future, because I believe You know what is best.

You know exactly what is right for me and exactly what is wrong me for me.

So I trust that in Your guidance and when following Your direction I am walking into what is best for me.

You have seen all things and You know what is to come.

In the name of Jesus I pray, Amen.

Dear Lord

I pray You keep me on Your path.

Father I need Your direction so I know where to go.

I cannot follow my own path because I will get lost.

If I follow my own path, I may walk into something dangerous, but when I walk on Your path I am protected.

Father help me to seek Your path and not my own path.

Because no matter how big and strong I am, Your path is always better than any other path, especially mine.

Help me lord I pray, I love You.

In the name of Jesus I pray, Amen.

Dear Lord

I pray for Your guidance.

I know that Your guidance leads to everything good, and great, and to happiness and peace and love.

Your guidance is the only way I can be somewhere good.

I pray that You lead me with Your guidance directing me to the good path.

I know that is only Your path which leads to greatness, and not any other.

Lord I pray that I have a great life, but that can only happen once I am following Your guidance and am on Your path.

I love You, keep me safe Father.

In the name of Jesus I pray, Amen.

Dear Lord

Thank You for Your wisdom.

I am praying for some help on making a decision.

I need Your help to decide on what choice to make, because I know that You have the correct answer.

When I come to You for my answer I know I can never go wrong.

Show me Lord and speak to me so I know what decision I should make and what option I should choose.

I trust in Your wisdom that Your choice is the right on for my life.

Thank You, I love You.

In the name of Jesus I pray, Amen.

Dear Lord

Thank You that You want to be a part of my journey.

Thank You for choosing me as Your child. Father, I pray You stay with me and guide me, every moment of my journey.

I love You Lord, and I am so pleased to be in your presence.

I am a special child, and all the praise goes to You Father.

Thank You for clearly laying a path before me, thank You that Your lightness leads the ways.

I cannot get lost from You, unless I walk another way.

Thank You for keeping me safe, and having a guard over me, as I walk towards You and You with me, and You completely in me.

It is so precious that I am able to follow You as Your child, and You as my father.

I love You. In the name of Jesus. Amen.

Dear Lord

I cannot walk my own journey.

I need You in every step that I take.

I pray You overcome me with Your presence Father.

I depend completely on You.

I can do nothing without You Father.

You are everything Father.

I thank You, that I can lean completely on You.

I thank You that I can completely follow You, and that Your direction is completely light. Your safety embraces me.

I will not walk without You Father, I pray You guide my every step and hold my feet up every step and moment.

I love You, in the name of Jesus I pray, Amen.

Dear Lord

God You rescued me, Jesus You are my saviour.

Father, I pray You guide me completely.

In any questions I have, I pray You answer me.

For every decision I have to make, Father I pray You reveal to me what choice I should make.

For every step of my life, completely lead me.

I love You and I thank You that I can call on You and ask these things.

The path to You is straight, and not everyone follows You.

But I will make sure that I follow You at all times, because I trust in You and I believe that You are the best option for me.

Everything You say Father, I will do because You know best.

I will not follow what I want and think is best, because You made me and You planned my life.

You know the best life I could ever want.

Thank You, I trust You and I love You.

In the name of Jesus I pray, Amen.

PRAYERS FOR GUIDANCE

Dear Lord

I trust You completely with my life and everything that is in it.

You created me and You know me.

Thank You for choosing me as Your child, I love You.

I pray for wisdom that I need to make decisions.

I pray that You provide me the wisdom to know what is wrong and what is right, and even what is nearly right.

For anything against Your word is wrong, and everything Your word says is right, as You are Your word, and Your word is truth.

I pray You guide me to tell other people of the truth and what is right.

Remove lies from my life I pray.

Thank You for being my light to follow, I love You.

In the name of Jesus I pray, Amen.

PRAYERS FOR PEACE

Dear Lord

Thank You for choosing me.

I am so proud to be able to call You my Father.

You are such a great God, and I am Your child.

You can do all things, thank You for making me feel safe knowing that You are in control of my life.

Because I have You, such a mighty Father, I have peace.

I do not need to worry about anything, because as a child of God I get special protection.

As a child of God, all things turn out to be great, because I have You as a Father.

Thank You that just being Your child and You being my Father, I can be happy that all will end well.

I pray that if I ever get worried that You remind me that I am Your child.

I love You Father, thank You.

In the name of Jesus I pray, Amen.

Dear Lord,

thank You for each second of the day.

I give You all the praise and the glory.

So amazing are You who created each second and each minute.

I trust You and my heart trusts You.

You know all things that have ever happened and all things that are to come.

I pray that I trust You with Your timing.

Lord You are in control of time, and I trust that Your timing is best.

I pray that I do not think that I have the best timing.

You know best when things should and should not happen.

I trust that You do all for my best benefit, so I can trust You with Your decisions.

I love You.

In the name of Jesus I pray, Amen.

PRAYERS FOR OTHER PEOPLE

Dear Lord

Please hear my prayers. I pray for my parents, and those who love after me.

I pray that You watch over them how You watch over me.

Thank You for those people who look after me and I pray You bless them with all Your heart.

Father, I pray that You enter each heart of those who look after me, and completely shine a light through them.

Father, I pray that You bring success and favour to all of those who look after me.

I pray that those who look after me are completely in love with You.

Father, I pray that those who love me are following You, so I pray they can be filled with wisdom and patience.

I pray that those who look after me walk in love and everything around them is love.

I pray that when we speak to each other, we speak in love.

I pray that any feelings that are not from love be removed now and forever.

Thank You Father, for those who look after me, I love them and I love You.

In the name of Jesus I pray, Amen.

PRAYERS FOR OTHER PEOPLE

Dear Lord

I pray for those who teach.

I thank You for those who teach me, I pray that You bless them and all that concerns them.

I pray You are strong in my teacher's hearts, I pray they do all things in Your image.

Thank You for their wisdom, I pray You shine through them and they get their wisdom through You.

I pray that You be the source for my teacher's knowledge, and lives.

I pray my teachers get completed by Your love.

I pray that You are the centre of their lives.

I pray that my teachers and I have a deep understanding of one another, I pray that You Father shine through all situations.

Bless my teachers with protection and patience.

I pray You keep their focus on You at all times, and do all of their teaching through love.

I pray You reward them richly, and show Your glory at all times.

Thank You for my precious teachers.

I love You.

In the name of Jesus I pray, Amen.

Dear Lord

I love You and give You the best thanks for all of my family.

Thank You for each family member and their value.

Father I pray that every one of my family members knows You strongly.

I pray You reveal Yourself to my family at all times, and shine Your face upon them.

I pray that You complete them, I pray You wrap them up completely in Your love.

Father I pray that You enter the hearts of my family and transform them into Your image.

I pray that all of my family walk in love.

I pray that we are a strong family, a family that can overcome hate with love, a family that can overcome bad with good.

I pray we are a family that are completely led and controlled by You Father.

I love You.

In the name of Jesus I pray, Amen.

PRAYERS FOR OTHER PEOPLE

Dear Lord

I thank You for my friends.

Father, I pray that You teach me to value each friend for the treasure they are.

I pray that each of my friends calls You their Father.

I pray You wrap each of my friends in Your arms of love and protection.

I pray that all of my friends can turn to You for healing, love, company and happiness.

I pray You pick them up if they fall down, and You show to them how much they can trust You.

I pray my friends depend on You.

I pray You speak to my friends and teach them to hear Your voice.

We are all Your children, so we are brothers and sisters in Your eyes.

And so in my eyes, also will I treat my friends as brothers and sisters.

I will forgive them and I will be a light.

Shine through me Father, so all who see me can see You.

I will be kind and open to my friends if they want to know You and I will always walk in love.

I love You.

In the name of Jesus I pray, Amen.

Dear Lord

Thank You for planning my journey.

I pray that You open doors for me.

I pray that You open doors of success for me to walk through.

I pray You open doors of opportunities for me.

I pray that You open doors for me on the path of righteousness, that I am able to go to the right place.

I pray that You open doors for me that I cannot open for myself, doors that are too heavy or big for me to open.

Thank You Father for opening these doors for me.

Thank You because even though I cannot open the doors on my own, You are right there to open the doors for me.

I love You.

In the name of Jesus I pray, Amen.

Dear Lord

Thank You for being my past, present and future.

I pray that You protect me at all times.

Father I pray that when I try to walk through doors which going in the wrong direction, that You close the doors for me.

Thank You for all of the times You have closed doors to protect me.

I pray that You close the doors which have been opened by other people, a door that You do not want me to go through.

I thank You for watching me at all times; I do not have to fear.

Father, I pray that You close the doors that even I may not want You to close.

I trust You know what doors I should be going through.

Even if want to go somewhere, I trust and believe that You know better than I do.

You know what is best for me, more than I do, because You know all things.

I love You.

In the name of Jesus I pray, Amen.

Dear Lord

I trust You completely with my future.

I will do everything that You want me to do Father, because You created me.

You know what I need and want, and what I was created for.

I pray that every moment I feel Your love in me, because it never leaves.

I pray that I act in love and trust in You, in the way that I love others and follow Your instructions.

I pray You reveal to me what You want in my life and what You would like me to do.

I pray You speak to me and show to me Your plans for me.

I will not think of my own plan, because it will not be right, and it will not match what I was created to do or was created for.

I will follow Your plan for my future, because You, being wise and smart, created it.

You know all things, and You will be with me when I walk on Your path.

Thank You for Your great plans for me, plans that I will love and love, thank You for being so sweet.

I love You.

In the name of Jesus I pray, Amen.

Dear Lord

I pray to be like You in all Your ways.

Jesus I pray that I have Your love, Your forgiveness, Your boldness, Your passion, Your truth and Your kindness.

I live each day in Your character and I pray You help me.

I thank You for everyday that You allow me to be more and more like You.

I pray that when other people see me, they see You in me.

I pray that each day I am closer to You.

Each and every day I pray I am more like You; I pray to grow to be closer to You.

There is nothing I want more than Your presence.

Each day of my life I pray You surround me with Your presence.

I thank You for each second You are here.

I thank You that I do not have to fear.

I want to see You and hear You each and every day.

I love You.

In the name of Jesus I pray, Amen.

Dear Lord

I pray that there is no evil or bad in this world.

Father I pray that You protect this world from anything bad that could happen.

As You are my shelter and my protector, I pray that You are the shelter for this world.

You are the strongest and You can do all things.

I pray for the world and that every person has a good heart and do joyful things.

I pray that every person is as sweet as You are Lord, and as sweet as I try to be.

I pray that every person in this world tries to be like You.

You are full of love, kindness, forgiveness and sweetness.

I pray that every person lives to be forgiving and sweet and kind, and that every person walks in love.

Thank You for listening to my prayers, I love You.

In the name of Jesus I pray, Amen.

Dear Lord

I pray for a rain of love in this world.

Father I pray that You pour out Your love onto this whole world.

I pray that no one misses out on Your love, but everyone gets touched.

Thank You for being such a loving God, that You want to love every person that ever exists.

Thank You for having such a big heart.

I pray that You fill every person in this world with a heart of love.

I pray You help everyone in this world to walk in love.

I pray that everyone is helpful, and sharing, and nice, and loving as You are Lord.

Thank You for You, thank You that Your love is in me every single moment.

I love You.

In the name of Jesus I pray, Amen.

NONE OTHER LIKE OUR GOD

Dear Lord

You fill me with absolute amazement.

Wow, I am in awe at Your awesomeness.

No one else could ever do what You.

You are on the highest level.

You are the one who created all things.

All things small and tiny, that my eyes cannot even see.

And You created things so big and huge that I can see from really far away.

You are so powerful and clever.

You created everything with such detail.

You created each eyelash on my eyelid.

You created every piece of grass that exists.

You are so careful and gentle, You make no mistakes.

You put so much care into each and every thing that You create.

Thank You and I love You.

In the name of Jesus I pray, Amen.

Dear Lord

You are such a smart, clever, intelligent God.

You created all of the seas and all of the sky.

You created the seasons and the weather.

You create the rain and the sun.

You create the clouds and the dust.

You give us all things, thank You it is so amazing.

You are so clever, and wonderful.

Everything I see is from You.

Everything I see around me is because of You.

Thank You my Father, I love You.

In the name of Jesus I pray, Amen.

Dear Lord

Thank You that I can trust You with all my heart.

There is no other like You so truthful in all of their ways, but You.

You are so trustworthy, You never ever lie and You never will.

Every word that is Yours is truth.

You always keep Your word, so I know You will never let me down.

I can trust in what You say and take it as facts, because You are so truthful.

I believe in Your every word, there is so much power.

Every single word You speak is truth, and anything that does not agree with Your word is not the truth, and I will not listen to it.

Thank You for being so honest with me, more honest than anyone I know.

I love You.

In the name of Jesus I pray, Amen.

Dear Lord

Thank You for Your very name.

There is no other like You. No one else compares.

There is so much power in the name of Jesus.

The very mention of the name Jesus and sickness cannot stay.

The mention of Jesus and sadness cannot remain.

Thank You Father for the name of Jesus.

No other name has such power.

No other name but Jesus has the power over all of the earth; nothing is the same at the sound of Jesus.

I love You Father, for Your sweetness.

The words in the bible bring life, the words in the bible are all truth, and the words in the bible are Your voice.

You speak to us through Your words Lord; no one else can do that.

You are amazing, thank You, for the gift of life.

I love You.

In the name of Jesus I pray, Amen.

Dear Lord

You are such a strong and mighty and powerful God.

You can do all things.

You can do the impossible.

You have done the impossible, thank You Father.

I pray that I see Your power in my life each and every day.

You can do all things that no one else could ever do, or even dream to do.

You are able to pick up a huge heavy gigantic mountain.

A mountain that I can see and also a mountain that is in my life.

Something that is huge and something that I cannot move in my life.

I thank You because You are able to move it.

You are able to lift me right up when I think I am falling.

You are able to open doors that I thought we're locked up tight.

Thank You, because anything that I can think of You can do and anything I ask of You I believe that You can do.

And if You think that it is good for me, I trust that You will do anything for me.

I love You.

In the name of Jesus I pray, Amen.

Dear Lord,

You were here before the world existed, You created the world.

You have always been here, and You always will be here.

You are always present and I pray You are a strong presence in my life.

Father, You have always existed and You will never leave.

Thank You Father for being reliable, You are always the same.

The same yesterday, today and tomorrow.

You are always love, You are always light, You are always truth and You are always life.

You are trust worthy because I can depend on You.

You never change Your mind, You never lie and You never go back on Your word.

Thank You for being a faithful God, You never let me down and You will never let me down.

I love You.

In the name of Jesus I pray, Amen.

Dear Lord

You are such a glorious God.

I give You all the honour and the praise and the glory.

There is no one like You.

The stars and sun and clouds and moon know Your name.

The sea knows You are glorious, and the sea listens to Your every command.

The trees know Your name, and listen to everything You say.

All the air that surrounds me is controlled by You; each blow of the wind is Your breath.

The entire world, everything that exists, knows You are glorious, and You are God to all.

You rule all things.

Thank You for choosing me to be Your child, and thank You I can call You my Father.

I love You.

In the name of Jesus I pray, Amen.

Dear Lord

You are my all.

You are like no other.

No other is like You.

You amaze me, I love You and thank You.

You are able to do all things.

You can give healing to anyone.

You can give life to anyone.

You can give happiness to someone who is very sad.

You can make someone happy, even if no one else can.

You can find someone who is lost, even if they are so lost they do not know where they are, You can show them the right direction.

You can fix someone whose heart is broken.

You are the perfect company for someone who is lonely.

You can make someone who is weak, very strong.

You can make someone who is shy very confident.

You can do all things.

I love You.

In the name of Jesus I pray, Amen.

Dear Lord

Thank You because victory is Yours.

All things are possible through You and by You.

Victory is always Yours.

Victory has always been Yours Father, from the start of existence and it will always be Yours through every area, and forever more.

I do not need to fear because victory is Yours, everything that I go through is Your battle Father, and You always win.

I trust You and believe You are powerful and mighty to win all things.

No one else is like You in all of Your ways.

I love You, and thank You for always being here for me.

In the name of Jesus, Amen.

Dear Lord

You are such a perfect wonder.

You are perfect in all You do and are.

There is no other that has never done wrong.

There is no other who speaks every single word of truth.

There is no other who knows all things that have ever happened or are to come.

There is no other more true to their word, no other who I can depend on and trust completely like You.

There is no other so sweet and loving, no other who forgives so much.

There is no other who thinks about me first, that will never ever and could never ever let me down.

There is no other who loves all people, no matter what.

There is no other who heals the sick, brings the dead to life and provides every breath.

There is no other like You.

You are the one and only, and I thank You so much that I get to call You my Father.

I love You for who You are.

I pray I never forget these things, but they stay in my heart.

In the name of Jesus I pray, Amen.

THE MOST IMPORTANT RELATIONSHIP

Dear Lord

As my Father, I know it is very important to always talk to You.

Thank You for always being here to listen and so I will always be happy to talk to You.

I know that I always talk to the people that I love, and I love You.

Even if I cannot see You, I can see You in other people and in myself.

I will talk to You about how my day has been, about all the good things that have happened and thank You for it.

I will give You all of my worries because I know that You care for me and will look after me and take them from me.

I will ask for the help for all of my worries, I will speak the answer and not the problem.

I will always make time to talk to You, how You always make time to listen to me.

Please help me if I want to talk to You, but I don't know what to say or how to say it. I will ask You for help and You will answer.

I will sing Your songs if words are too much.

I love You, and so I will talk to You always, in all ways, all days.

In the name of Jesus I pray, Amen.

Dear Lord

I will always listen to You.

I pray for open ears at all times.

When You speak to me through people or words or thoughts I will listen.

I will not ignore You.

When You tell me what to do I will follow what You say.

You say You love me, I am wonderfully made, I must love and forgive everyone.

I must respect my parents, I must help people.

Nothing shall hurt me, You are my shield.

I listen to all of these things and I will follow them.

If I want to do something that is the opposite of what You have told me, I pray You help stop me.

I pray that I will think about how much I love You, and how I never want You to be sad with me.

Father, please forgive me if I have ever ignored You and if I ever do, and thank You.

I love You.

In the name of Jesus I pray, Amen.

Dear Lord

Thank You for all things.

I am so grateful to have You as my Father that I can always turn to.

I thank You that I am Your child and You will always look after me and protect me.

I thank You Father for every breath You give me; I owe it all to You.

I thank You Father for every person that loves me, and for every person I love.

Thank You Father for everything that I own, it is all because of You.

I am very blessed and I thank You Lord.

At all times I give You praise.

If I am ever sad, I will give You thanks and be happy in the fact I have You and You will always be here.

Thank You for Your son Jesus, that You so love us You gave him to us.

Thank You Jesus that You came down to us and gave up everything because You love us.

Thank You for my every second chance.

You give me life Father.

I love You, and give You thanks.

In the name of Jesus I pray, Amen.

Dear Lord

I am so proud to be Your child, and I am so proud to call You my Father.

I will always be proud of You, how You are proud of me.

Father I am proud to always call You when I need some help and some guidance.

I am proud to say You are the best ever, because You are.

You can do all things.

I know You will always open doors that are good for me and always close doors that are bad for me.

I am proud to tell others how much I love You and tell others how much You love me.

I am proud that everyone knows, You are my number one!

You are mine, and I am Yours.

I love You Father.

In the name of Jesus I pray, Amen.

Dear Lord

I love You so so so much!

My Father, my everything, my heart pours out love for You.

There is no other like You.

I love You with every little part of me.

I love You for who You are.

You are love, peace, joy, forgiveness, trust, dependable, protector, provider, and the list goes on and on.

I love You for who I am because of You; I am strong, happy, bold, alive, and free.

You created me in Your image, and so You make everything You are.

I love You because of all You have given me, people who love me, clothes, food, shelter, warmth, water.

I love You always Lord.

I will live in my love for You by doing what You say, seeking You each and every day and giving praise at all times.

If I ever feel low in love for You I can just look around and see You in all things great.

Thank You Lord, I love You.

In the name of Jesus I pray, Amen.

Dear Lord

As my Father I look up to You.

I will respect You at all times because You are the biggest and the best.

You are so mighty and strong, I am amazed.

You are so loving and sweet, I am joyful.

You are so good and honest, I want to be like You.

You can see all things and do all things.

You are everywhere all at once, Wow! And You are my Father.

I will listen to You and do as You say, because as You told me to respect my parents,

I respect You.

I give thanks to You for everything because You give me everything.

I love You, in the name of Jesus I pray, Amen.

Dear Lord

Thank You for choosing me, I love You.

I pray You teach me what it means to me Your child.

I pray You fill me with the knowledge and boldness to live as Your child.

Thank You that I can come to You as Your child, and like my carers You completely look after me.

You love me more than anyone else.

You only want what is best for me.

As Your child it means I can come to You in times of need.

As a faithful Father and an almighty God, You help me at all times, any time in every way.

You are so kind to me, thank You, I love You.

In the name of Jesus I pray, Amen.

Dear Lord

I pray that You reveal the boldness that is within me, because You are within me.

I thank You that I can talk to You and ask You all things.

I pray You show me that I can ask You for help for anything at all.

My trust in You is high, thank You.

I have seen Your love and so I trust You.

Thank You for always helping me, I open up my heart to let You change me into what You want me to be.

Thank You because I trust You to make the best changes.

I open up my heart to hear You and see You.

I cannot be closed with You, but in everything, I pray that I am open to You.

I share everything that I am with You, because even though You know everything about me, I will still tell You anyway.

When I share with You, I thank You that You talk back to me.

I love You.

In the name of Jesus I pray, Amen.

Dear Lord

Thank You for Your word.

Thank You that You provide to me everything I need to know about You in the precious bible.
I will treasure the bible with all my heart, because it has everything You are; Your character and Your instructions.

The bible is the word and the word is Jesus, and the word is truth, power and love.

Thank You, because I find love and the truth in the bible.

Thank You because everything I need is in the bible.

Thank You for all of the instructions in the bible, so I know how to live.

Thank You for all of the advice so I know how to deal with everything.

Thank You for the love that is in the bible, all of Your words of love and encouragement.

Thank You for the power in the bible, Your word overcomes all things.

Jesus overcomes all things.

Thank You for Your truth, I will trust the bible as Your words.

I will base all my decisions on the bible, as Your word.

Thank You because I can find Your word in the bible.

Thank You for the easy access I have to the bible.

I love You.

In the name of Jesus I pray, Amen.

Dear Lord

Thank You for the time You give me.

Like how I make time for family and friends, I will make time for You.

I will put special times in my day to spend time with You.

I will give You time, and I pray nothing gets in the way.

I pray that I do not let people take that time from me, or choose to give it away.

Father, You are the most important to me, so I give You my time, which You have given me.

You give me every second of my life, thank You.

I want to spend time with You because I love You, and I enjoy Your presence.

When I come to spend time with You I will not be focused on something else, but I pray I will talk to You directly.

Thank You Father that You really want to spend time with me, I love You so much.

In the name of Jesus I pray, Amen.

ALL ABOUT JESUS

Dear Lord

Thank You for Your precious Son Jesus.

Jesus Christ, my Lord and my Saviour, my king.

Jesus I worship You, the one who has always been and will always be.

Jesus, thank You, You have always existed, You are the true word of our living God.

God's word is truth, and truth is what You are Jesus.

God's word is never changing, and Jesus I thank You for never changing.

God's word has always been with God, God's word is God.

Jesus You are God and God is You.

Our Father in heaven, and Jesus, You are our Father's Son in heaven.

Father, Son and the sweet Holy Spirit, always and forever, together You make God.

I am in awe, I love You.

In the name of Jesus I pray, Amen.

Thank You, Father in heaven.

Thank You for the sweet precious gift of Your Son, Jesus.

Father You gave up Your Son Jesus so that You might save us.

Thank You Father, I love You.

You so love us that You let Your Son come to earth, so that he could save all of us.

Thank You Father.

No one else but God has ever loved us so much, thank You.

I pray I will live out my thanks by the way I live my life.

Showing my love by appreciating that I have You and for all You have done for us.

Thank You for filling me up, I love You.

In the name of Jesus I pray, Amen.

Dear Lord

Thank You God for such a perfect Jesus.

Jesus, You have never done anything wrong, ever.

You are God and You cannot do evil.

Even on earth You did no wrong or evil.

Thank You for submitting completely to our Father.

Even though there were so many people against You, You were still perfect.

Perfectly kind, perfectly patient, perfectly generous, perfectly loving, perfectly strong.

Even though You did no wrong, You died for us.

Thank You Jesus, thank You saviour.

You saved the world by the sacrifice of Your perfect death.

We have all done something that we should not have, or have not done something that we should have, but yet You went on our behalf.

Thank You.

I love You.

In the name of Jesus I pray, Amen.

Dear Lord

Thank You for Your Son Jesus Christ.

Jesus You overcame the whole entire world.

When You died for us, You rose up after three days and walked on earth.

Jesus You overcame death.

Nothing can hold You Jesus.

Nothing has a hold or power over You Jesus.

Jesus, when You died for us You took control and authority.

I thank You for Your sacrifice, and I love You.

Thank You because when You overcame death, You overcame everything else.

I love You.

In the name of Jesus I pray, Amen

Dear Lord

Thank You Jesus for being such a beautiful example.

You are perfect.

Father, I pray You always lead me to follow the same path as Jesus.

Jesus You are our direction, the direction is straight to You Father.

Jesus You lived each day on earth as an example, You followed everything that our Father asked of You.

I pray I live my life in the same way as You Jesus.

I pray I follow everything that our Father asks me to do. Jesus lived on earth in love.

Jesus, You loved no matter who, where or what.

I pray I follow example and live in love, loving all people.

Jesus You lived on earth to serve and help others, I pray I follow example and live to give and help.

In the name of Jesus I pray, Amen.

Dear Lord

Thank You for Jesus.

Jesus, thank You for Your perfect self.

Thank You Jesus for following our Father and submitting completely to Him.

Thank You Jesus for Your life, and that You gave up Your life for us.

Even though You have never done any wrong, even on earth as a man.

You are God, You are perfect, and love us so much that You gave up Your life to save us.

You saved us from separation with God.

Thank You Jesus for Your sweet sacrifice, on the cross, that You did only for us.

You sacrificed so that we receive complete health, freedom and success.

Thank You Jesus that Your heart thought of all of us, each and every person.

I love You.

In the name of Jesus I pray, Amen.

Dear Lord

Thank You Jesus.

Thank You God for Your word.

Your word is truth, love, perfect, comforting, and Jesus You are God's word.

Thank You Jesus, for Your power.

Jesus, I pray that I follow Your example as a child of God.

A Son who knows that God's word has power over every and all things, You did not speak unless He told You to.

I pray I will use God's word in my life.

Thank You Father for the opportunity to read Your word and know Your word.

I pray I will use Your word to get through all situations.

I trust in Your word and in Your power I trust that if I speak something out loud, it will happen if it is good for me.

I will use Your word as the truth and apply it in my life as truth.

As Jesus faced even the really bad times, He used God's word to overcome.

Because God's word is truth and love, and nothing can win against truth and love.

In the name of Jesus I pray, Amen.

Dear Lord

Thank You Jesus.

Thank You for Your love Jesus and all You are.

Thank You Jesus because You are love.

On earth You walked in love, and everything You are is love and everything about love is You.

Father, I pray that You help me to walk in love in all things that I do.

God Your word is love.

Jesus thank You, You loved all people, even if others did not.

You cared for all people even if they were not where they should be, but by believing in You they discovered the way to You.

Thank You.

In the name of Jesus I pray, Amen.

Dear Lord

Thank You Jesus for being our freedom.

Jesus it is because of You that we are free from pain, and sadness and darkness.

Thank You Jesus, for making us free from doing bad things.

You have transformed us to be everything You are.

No other Jesus like You.

There is power in the name of Jesus, and so I will use Your name Jesus at all times.

When I need freedom, I will call on You Jesus to set me free.

Thank You that I can call out Your name Jesus.

Because of You Jesus we are free to be with our Father in heaven.

Because of You Jesus it is not about what we do but who we are.

Thank You because I am not perfect, but I am a child of God, and so I love and trust You God.

I welcome You into my heart and let You transform me be to be like You.

Thank You, I love You.

In the name of Jesus I pray, Amen.

Dear Lord

Thank You Jesus for being our direction and door, to have a relationship with our Father in heaven.

If it was not for You Jesus, we would not be able to have conversations with our Father or have the Holy Spirit deep within us.

You made a path Jesus, thank You for the door You have opened and the wall You knocked down.

You tore the barrier between people and our Father in heaven.

If it was not for You Jesus, I would not be able to hear the sweet voice of God every day.

If it was not for You Jesus, I would not be able to feel God wrap me in His arms every day.

I would not have the peace, or love, or joy, or courage I have today.

Thank You Jesus, You have allowed us to have a deep relationship with our Father in heaven.

And our relationship is what my life is focused around.

I love You.

In the name of Jesus I pray, Amen.

A FRIEND IN GOD

Dear Lord

Thank You for Your presence in my life.

Thank You Father that I can speak to You all the time, any time and every time that I need to.

Thank You for listening to everything I have to say to.

You always listen; You are never too busy for me.

You always have time for me, no matter what.

I can spend forever and ever talking to You and You will never get bored.

You are the best listener.

I can speak to You about anything at all and You will always know what I mean.

Even when I cannot quite explain it, or when my words do not come out right.

You hear me even when I do not speak at all.

You know what I want to say even when I do not say anything at all.

You are such a good listener and I am so thankful that You my Father will always and forever listen to me.

I love You.

In the name of Jesus I pray, Amen

A FRIEND IN GOD

Dear Lord

You are such a good friend to me.

You are so kind to me.

You treat me so well.

No one treats me as good as You.

You are so gentle and lovely and sweet.

I know that any time and every time someone is kind to me it is You being kind, through them, to me.

You are such a kind God.

Every sweet word You speak, my heart fills with joy.

You always make me feel welcome God, You never shut me out.

You always make me feel comfortable to say everything that is on my heart.

Thank You Lord for being so kind to me.

I love You.

In the name of Jesus I pray, Amen.

Dear Lord

Thank You Father for Your loving protection over my life and over all that has to do with me.

Thank You for keeping me safe from everything.

I trust Your protection and Your promise that nothing shall ever harm me.

You wrap me up with Your warm arms and keep me hidden in Your love.

You are my safety and in You I find my protection.

You see all things, Your watchful eyes are looking out for me, and so You protect me from things that I cannot even see.

There is no one like You.

You are so powerful and mighty, You are stronger than anyone else and so You win everything.

I am so proud to have You as my Father and my protector.

I love You.

In the name of Jesus I pray, Amen.

Dear Lord

Thank You for being such a great provider.

You provide me every single thing I need.

Even the things I do not know that I need, You provide.

Even when I want something, You know if it will be good or bad for me, because You know best.

And if what I want is bad for me I have to trust You, because You know everything about me; even more than I know myself.

And if what I want is good for me, then I will trust in Your timing when I will receive these things.

I pray I learn to wait until when You think it is best for me, and not when I think it is best.

Thank You for being such an amazing provider, I love You Lord.

In the name of Jesus I pray, Amen.

Dear Lord

Thank You for being such a great helper in my life.

You help me in every situation.

And Your help is the best kind of help that I could ever receive.

Father You do the impossible.

You do things so amazing.

I cannot even count how many things You have done, I would continue forever and ever. Because of this, I know You can help me in any and every thing.

There is nothing too big for my God and nothing too small that You will not help me with.

I pray for Your help Lord, I need Your help, and I am asking You because You give the best help.

I need You to show me what to do and how to do it.

I need Your great power to help me do something I cannot do by myself.

I need Your mighty hands to help me do something that no one else can help me with.

I trust in You to help me Lord, and I remember all the times You have helped me before.

Thank You Lord, I love You.

In the name of Jesus I pray, Amen.

Dear Lord

You are my comforter.

You wrap me up in Your care and Your love.

You rescue me when I am sad, and lift me up into Your bright light.

You feel every pain I feel and You wipe away every tear.

You soothe every pain I feel with Your love.

I am so happy in Your arms; there is nowhere else I want to be.

Each frown I have You turn it upside down to a smile with Your care. You open Your arms to hug me and You let me know I can always lean on You Lord.

You are always there to give me comfort, at any hour on any day.

Even late at night or early in the morning You are always there to comfort me.

You provide the best ever comfort, You know just how to look after me.

You heal my heart, if it is ever broken.

You know where the pieces of my heart are and You pick them up and put them back together again.

Thank You Father, I love You so much.

In the name of Jesus I pray, Amen.

Dear Lord

Your love is so beautiful.

Thank You for always loving me.

You are my best friend, You are so lovely.

Your love pours on me like rain and it warms me up like the sun.

Your love is beautiful like the nature.

Your love never stops; it is like a clock that keeps going on and on.

Your love is so huge!

Your love is bigger than any mountain; Your love is wider than any ocean.

Your love reaches everyone at all times, in all ways.

There is nothing more powerful than Your love.

Your love can do all things; Your love can do the impossible.

You love me more than anyone else can, because Your heart is so big.

Your love is so sweet and gentle.

I love You so much Father, You are my favourite.

There is no one else like You. Keep me forever safe in Your love.

In the name of Jesus I pray, Amen.

Dear Lord

Please forgive me for every naughty thing I have done and for every good thing I did not do.

It is a new day and I will change to do what You would like me to do Lord.

I pray I will follow Your example of being such a perfect Father.

I pray I will not complain if I am told off because I know it is only out of love, and because I should be the best I was created to be.

You created me amazing and I am amazing.

Please Lord, help me to be amazing and to do good and to not do bad.

Even when I don't feel like it, I pray that You will help me to, because You are such a loving Father.

I will be good because I love You back.

In the name of Jesus I pray, Amen.

Dear Lord

Thank You for being so faithful.

You always keep to Your word and You never let me down.

You only make promises You can stick to.

You never fail on Your promises.

I trust You completely, because You only speak truth.

Oh faithful Lord, I look up to You as my example.

You are everything I want to be, You are wonderful.

I can depend on You completely because I know that I can only expect the best, as Your word says.

Even if other people let me down I must forgive them and know that You never let me down.

Even if I feel like what You promised is very hard, even if it looks like what You promised is very hard, I will always believe in my heart and know in my mind that You can never let me down.

It is not possible for You to let me down because You are so faithful.

I will always have You, thank You.

I love You.

In the name of Jesus I pray, Amen.

Dear Lord

Thank You for always being here for me.

You are here for me every second, of every minute, of every hour, of every day of my life.

I am so happy to have You with me always.

You are here for me in the middle of the night, past bedtime, even when I am sleeping.

You are here for me if I wake up in the night, and You look after me.

You are here for me even in the very early morning, before everyone wakes up, even before the birds outside open their eyes.

You never leave me.

Even if I cannot see anyone else around me, I know that You are here Father.

You always have time for me.

You are here for me in the happy times and in the sad times, in funny times and in the scary times.

You are always here for me. I love You.

In the name of Jesus I pray, Amen.

LOVING OTHERS

Dear Lord

Every one of Your children is my brother and sister.

I pray I will treat them as such.

I pray I will pour out my heart, and give sweet words. I pray I will pick other people up when they are down.

I pray I will be company for those who are alone.

I pray I will say sorry if I have done wrong, and will accept someone's apology if they have done wrong to me.

Thank You Jesus that You have put inside me a big heart.

My heart is big enough to love all people, as You do Father.

Thank You and I love You.

I pray for the courage and boldness to stand up for other people and I pray for the wisdom to know how to do it Your way.

Father, I am listening to hear You. Speak to me, I pray, and give me guidance.

Everyone is my brother and sister in Christ, and so I will treat them that way.

In the name of Jesus I pray, Amen.

Dear Lord

I thank You for my soul.

My soul is my emotions, mind and choices.

My soul is everything I think and the reason of everything I do.

I pray You take control of my soul, to make my soul be like what You want my soul to be like.

I pray I can be how You want me to be Lord.

A soul is so valuable.

Father I know You want to help as many souls be how they were created to be.

Thank You for protecting my soul, You can only look after it if I give You permission to.

A soul is so very, very, very precious.

A soul cannot be bought; anything offered for a soul is of no value.

A soul is worth more than even the best car, a soul is more worthy than the best toy, a soul is more precious than the best ever shoes!

My soul is so precious, thank You God.

I will treasure it and let You protect it for me.

I love You.

In the name of Jesus I pray, Amen.

Dear Lord

Please forgive me.

I pray for help to forgive others, as You have asked me to do so, and to forgive how You forgive me.

I will forgive others because I love others. It is in my heart to be a loving person to every single person, even if I am unhappy with someone.

Your love in me is stronger than any hate that is in me or is around me.

Your love can do all things Lord, and I thank You that Your love is in me.

I can overcome all bad things with good.

If someone has made me feel bad or sad I will tell them, I will tell someone else I trust and I will tell You Lord.

Once I tell You Lord, You will sort it out, so I no longer need to be upset.

When I trust You to let You know my problems, I pass them on to You and that means they leave me.

Because I believe in You, that You are strong and powerful to deal with my problems, but I am not.

Thank You Lord, I love You.

In the name of Jesus I pray, Amen.

Dear Lord

You are so so good to me.

You are good all the time.

You are good to me even when I do not deserve it.

You are good to me even when I do not realise.

You such a good God, such a good Father.

The same way You are good to me Father I pray to be good to others.

Even when I think that other people do not deserve me to be good to them, I pray to be good to them, because I am a child of God and You live in me Lord.

I will be good to other people even if they do not say please or thank You.

I will be good to people even if I do not get anything back.

I will be good to every person, not just the people that I really like, but even to the people I do not like.

Because You love everyone and You live in me, so I must love everyone.

I pray I will do good things all the time.

I pray people will know it is because I am a child of God, and You live in me Father.

I love You.

In the name of Jesus I pray, Amen.

Dear Lord

Thank You for all of Your help and thank You for making me excellent!

You are excellent, and all Your children are excellent, because You have made them in Your image.

If someone does something that You would not like I pray I do not talk badly about them, but will help them.

Father, because You are in me, I pray I will be the help to others the same way You are the help to me.

So through me Lord You will be their help.

For no one can judge anyone, except You God.

Because no one is perfect but You God.

I cannot judge others because they do not know what is right, I have to help them and tell them what is right.

I have to help with my love, not hate, because love overcomes everything.

Thank You Father for Your love and I pray that I use Your love to help others.

In the name of Jesus I pray, Amen.

Dear Lord

I pray to not let bad things come out of my mouth.

I pray to not talk rudely about someone, I will love everyone when they are there and even when they are not there.

If I hear someone talking badly about someone else I will not be a part of it but I pray to help them, and ask how they can help the person instead.

I will speak words of light at all times, thank You.

You can hear me at all times Lord, I pray to only say things that are pleasing to Your ears.

I will at all times say sweet words, because You always speak the same about me, to me and in heaven at all times.

I trust in You.

In the name of Jesus I pray, Amen.

LOVING YOURSELF

Dear Lord

Thank You for choosing me as Your child.

I will love myself because I have been chosen by You carefully.

You found me and You love me.

It means the most to me that I am Your child, thank You.

I pray to treat all of Your children as treasure, me included.

I pray to live as everything You want me to live like.

Thank You for making me caring and loving, like You are.

Thank You for making me wise, that I know to follow You, in all of Your ways.

Thank You for making me beauty in Your eyes, that I am beautiful deep inside and outside.

I love You Father.

In the name of Jesus I pray, Amen.

Dear Lord

You are wonderful.

Thank You for each breath You give me and each moment I have to be in Your presence.

You are a wonderful Father and I thank You and love You for how You created me.

Every part of me was created by You Father, and so I will love every part of me.

It does not matter what anyone else has to say.

I was created wonderfully, because I was created by a wonderful God.

I will love myself because I love You and You love me.

In the name of Jesus I pray, Amen.

Dear Lord

You are amazing.

Father, You amaze me at how You have made all of the people in this world.

There are so many people and You created each and every one.

Thank You for Your time that You took to create each person.

Thank You for creating me in such an interesting way that I am like no one else.

Thank You for creating me in such an amazing way that I am able to do what some people cannot do.

Thank You Father for gifting me with the skills I have, I can do special things with the hands You have given me.

You are truly amazing, thank You.

I love You Father.

In the name of Jesus I pray, Amen.

Dear Lord

You are so perfect. You make no mistakes and You do everything for a reason.

I admire You because You have no faults and You do everything as You plan.

Father, thank You for making me.

I trust that You made me exactly how You want me to be, because You make no mistakes, and I am how I was meant to be.

I pray to learn that even if there is something different about me from someone else, it is for a reason and I trust in You that it was not a mistake but on purpose.

I know that You know the best life for me, and You want the best life for me and You have planned the best life for me.

All I need to do is follow You and I will experience the best life, I love You.

In the name of Jesus I pray, Amen.

Dear Lord

Thank You for creating me special.

Thank You that I am special from everyone else.

I pray I understand that everyone is made different from every other person.

I love You Father for the way You created me.

I am happy because of how special You made me.

There is something special about me: about the way I walk, about the way I talk, about the way I think, about the way I act.

There is something special in me that is not like anyone else.

I pray that I do not want to be a copy of anyone else, because You made me to be different from everyone else.

Thank You for making me different Lord.

I love You.

In the name of Jesus I pray, Amen.

Dear Lord

I love You very much.

Thank You for creating me for a reason.

There is a reason that I was made, and Father I pray You let me know what it is.

The reason You made me is to complete a very special task and live in a very special way; it is a different reason to anyone else.

Every single person has a different reason for being made, and it is not the same.

I will be happy with whatever reason, and I will follow Your direction so that I can live out my life in that reason.

I pray that You will show me and speak to me, and let me know when I am ready for the reason You made me.

I love You.

In the name of Jesus I pray, Amen.

Dear Lord

I love who You made me to be.

You created me in Your image and I pray to live in every way how You are.

I love me because I love who You are, and You made me like You.

I pray to follow in the way You act Father, because You made me to act how You act. You made me to speak how You speak, so I will live to speak with Your words.

Father, everything that You do I must seek to do also.

I really love You and I admire You and I give You all the praise.

Thank You for creating me in Your image, You make it possible for me to live like You and be like You.

I love You.

In the name of Jesus I pray, Amen.

Dear Lord

Thank You that there is no one like me.

You have created me to be one in a million.

Even if I look like someone else there is no one else like me.

Even if I sound like someone else, there is no one else like me.

You have created me so carefully that there will never be anyone like me.

Thank You for spending so long to create me.

You know how many hairs are on my head and how many eyelashes I have.

You are an amazing Father, I love You very much.

There is no one else who would spend so much time on me, thank You for creating me so carefully.

I love You.

In the name of Jesus I pray, Amen.

Dear Lord

Thank You for making me so valuable.

I pray to understand how valuable I am to You and to other people.

I pray that I am able to see what a treasure I am.

I should treat myself very gently because I am so rare, and a wonderful gift.

I am far more valuable than diamonds or rubies or gems.

Thank You for making me very treasured, more exciting than a treasure chest.

I am filled with more than gold or silver, because I am filled with You Lord.

I am filled up to the top with You Lord, until I overflow.

Thank You for making me very precious, like no other.

I love You.

In the name of Jesus I pray, Amen.

Dear Lord

Thank You for Your time.

Thank You Father for the time and care You took to make me.

Because I love You and I am very thankful, I will make sure that I look after me.

I will make sure that I treat myself well with just enough of everything that I need.

I will make sure that in everything that I do I am very careful, so I do not hurt myself, hurt what You created.

I will give myself the best, because I deserve the best as a child of God, and I will make sure I do all things in love.

I pray to follow Your guidance on how to look after myself, treating myself as precious as I am.

I love You.

In the name of Jesus I pray, Amen.

MADE IN GOD'S IMAGE

Dear Lord

I was created in Your image and I pray to walk in it.

I was created with a big heart filled with love.

You are such a kind loving Father and so I will walk in love.

Everywhere I go I pray to spread love.

I pray to share the love You have given me.

I will share love through my words and through my actions.

I will give extra love for those who really need it.

I will give lots of smiles, and share what I have.

I will help people when they are struggling and not exclude anyone, or make anyone feel alone.

Thank You Lord for Your love, I will share it with everyone, everywhere I go.

I love You.

In the name of Jesus I pray, Amen.

Dear Lord

Thank You for choosing me to be Your child.

I am very proud to call You my Father and very proud to be Your child.

I pray everyone who knows me will know that I am a child of God.

When I talk about what makes me who I am, I will share about how Your love makes me complete.

When someone is sad I will tell them how Your light lifts me up.

When someone is scared I will tell them how You keep me safe in Your arms, and trusting in You I am brave.

When someone needs help, I will tell them how You give the best help; and You can do all things, and I can do all things through Jesus.

When someone thinks they are missing something I will tell them how there is no one better than You and You are always here for us.

You always have time for us.

When someone is ill I will tell them how You are a healer and that praying in the name of Jesus is healing.

I will tell them how You never lie, always tell the truth and never let me down.

I will always surround myself with people who love You as much as I love You.

Because I only want to be surrounded by Your love.

In the name of Jesus I pray, Amen.

Dear Lord

You are absolutely excellent and everything You do is done perfectly.

So I pray to walk in Your image and be as excellent as I was created to be.

I will always try my hardest in everything that I do; I will give 110% effort at all times.

I will always finish what I start.

Lord give me strength to finish all that I do until the end.

I will not give up and I will not quit.

Even if it is hard I pray for Your help to the end.

And because I walk in excellence, I will always help others to be excellent as well.

I will help people and support people.

When others feel like they want to give up I will cheer them on to the finish line.

Father, You created us all differently and so I know that different people will be really good at different things.

So I may not be as good at something as someone else, but as long as I try my hardest and do all I can do, then I am excellent!

I am a child of God and I was created perfectly to be excellent.

Thank You, I love You.

In the name of Jesus I pray, Amen.

Dear Lord

You love me so much and I love You too.

I will always love You, my heart is for You Lord, and I give You 100% of me because You created 100% of me.

I will always make time to talk to You Father, even if I have a lot to do, because You always have time for me.

I will always make sure that I listen to You as much as I talk to You, because I don't want to miss what You have to say.

I will always love myself, as I was created because You created me perfectly.

I pray to always love others as I love myself because You created them.

I will always do as You say and let You lead me Lord.

No matter what it looks like and no matter what it feels like I will always trust in You Father because You protect me and You know me best.

I love You.

In the name of Jesus I pray, Amen.

Dear Lord

You are so powerful.

With Your words You created every single thing that exists.

I was created in Your image and so what I say has a lot of power.

I pray to not say anything bad, but I will only say good things.

I pray to be nice to everyone with my words.

I will always say hello and goodbye.

I will always say thank You and welcome.

I will always say sorry if I have been wrong.

I will think before I speak, and ask if it a good thing to say.

Everything I say has power, and so I will speak into life things that I may not see yet.

I declare only good things over me and everyone else I know.

I am happy, I am loved, I am brave, I am strong, I am wonderful and I am light.

I love You Lord.

In the name of Jesus I pray, Amen.

Dear Lord

In everything that I do, I pray I do well.

I pray to be as good as You are.

I will be kind and use my manners.

I will help people when they need help.

I will not be rude or mean, or make anyone feel bad.

I will make everyone feel happy and loved.

I will follow what You tell me to do, and I will do as I am told at all times.

You are such a good Father and You are all things right.

I will follow You and do the things that You do.

I will listen to the instructions of those who look after me and I will listen to the instructions of the teachers I have.

I will think about something before I do it.

If I know I am about to do something bad, Father I pray I stop, and take a moment to ask myself what You would want me to do.

I do not want to do anything that will make You unhappy.

I want to be good because it will make You happy.

Thank You. And because You are in me, I am good, and I do good things.

In the name of Jesus I pray, Amen.

Dear Lord

As Your child I will be an example to everyone, how You are an example to me.

You love me, and so I will love everyone to let them know that we should all love each other.

You forgive me, and so I will also forgive everyone, to let people know we should not hold anything bad in our heart.

You are good and so I am good.

So even when other people are doing something naughty, even if it looks fun, I will not join in.

I will be an example of how amazing You are, because You are the answer to everything.

I will do good so that people know what good is.

I will thank You for everything, so everyone knows what a loving Father You are.

I will let people know that putting You first, talking and listening to You, loving You, trusting You and following You are the most important things.

I will live as an example of what it means to be Your child.

I love You.

In the name of Jesus I pray, Amen.

Dear Lord

Thank You because Jesus on earth was a perfect being.

I pray to be perfect like You, Sweet Jesus, You cared for others more than Yourself.

Even though You are perfect and most Holy, and worthy to be praised and adored You did absolutely everything for us.

Thank You Jesus. It did not matter when it was, Jesus You helped.

I was created in Your image God, and so like Jesus I pray to take care of other people.

I pray that my heart desires to help and care for other people.

I pray that everything I do is to please You and to help people.

In the name of Jesus I pray, Amen.

Dear Lord

I am Your child, You have chosen me and You love me.

Thank You.

I love You, You are my Father.

I will live each day to be perfect in Your image, for You are completely perfect.

I pray to be as loving and giving and generous.

If I have a lot I will share it out to everyone, for You give me all things.

Even I do not have a lot; I will give to those who need more than I do.

I pray You put inside me the love to do these things, because I cannot do it by myself, I need You.

You are a Father of grace and love.

You love at all times Lord, no matter what.

I pray that I love at all times no matter what.

You are a great and kind Father, and I love You and thank You, as through You I can be perfect.

In the name of Jesus I pray, Amen

Dear Lord

You are a helper of those in need.

You always make time and You have a pure heart.

It does not matter who we are, when we call out to You, You help us.

I pray I can be like You.

I pray that I will always find someone to help.

For I live to do what You want Lord, and I need You to help me.

I will always be available to turn to for help, my heart will be big.

No matter who it is, even if they are not my friend, I will help someone.

If someone is in need I will try to provide.

Thank You for the heart full of love You have given me.

I love You.

In the name of Jesus I pray, Amen.

MY FAVOURITE BIBLE STORIES

This book is dedicated to Alexander 'King' Paul, a beautiful, precious and inspirational child of God who was taken from us much too soon.

Special Thanks to:
Pastor Patrick Cross
&
Pastor Jennifer Moore (Armour of Truth ministry)

Written by: Barbara Walters-Ennis, Ricky Senior & Janice Price
Design by: Kelly Nicholls
Edited by: Jamilla Evans & Barbara Walters-Ennis

Printed on recyclable products (ie paper)
Printed in China

CONTENTS

THE OLD TESTAMENT

The New Testament

The Creation of Earth

(Genesis 1: 1-31, 2:13)

In the beginning, before God created earth there was total darkness. One day God said 'let there be light' and all of a sudden there was light, which God decided was good, so he separated the light from the darkness. God decided to call the light 'Day' and the darkness 'Night' and before the night there was the evening and after the night there was the morning and this was the first day.

God then decided to divide the waters from the rest of the earth and he created the sky, which he called heaven. When God separated the waters from the dry land he called the land earth and the waters, Seas and God knew that this was good.

God then commanded the land to bring forth grass, herbs, seed, trees and fruit and He created the seasons, Winter Spring, Summer and Autumn, which would be the signs to show the days, months and the years.

On the fourth day God went further and created the stars to shine over the earth and to divide the darkness from the light.

The following day God commanded the waters to bring forth life and he created fishes large and small that could swim in shallow waters as well as in the ocean. He then created a variety of birds that could fly above the earth. God blessed all the living creatures and told them to go forth and multiply and they obeyed God.

By the sixth day God made animals large and small such as sheep, cows, lions, rabbits tigers, bears and elephants to roam the land. He also created spiders that crawled on the earth and when God looked around him he was happy, but he thought that there was something that was missing. God decided that he would create man in his own image to rule over everything in the land and the seas.

God created the whole earth with everything in it within six days and on the seventh day God rested.

This story reminds us how without God there would be no earth, no birds, no animals, no fishes and no people. It also reminds us that like God we need to take one day out of the week to rest and praise God for what he has done for us.

The Story of Adam and Eve

(Genesis 2:4-25, 3:1-15)

After God had made all the animals on earth, he decided that he needed to make a man to be in charge of all the animals.
The man that God made was called Adam. God brought all the animals and the birds and fishes to Adam and told him to give them all names and whatever Adam called them from then on that was their name.

God soon recognised that Adam was lonely and so he took out one of Adam's ribs and made a partner for Adam, a woman called Eve.

God put Adam and his partner Eve to live in a beautiful garden, which was called the Garden of Eden. There were lots of beautiful trees in the Garden of Eden with a variety of tasty and juicy fruits.

God told Adam and Eve that they must cultivate the land in the garden and that they could freely eat. However there was one tree in the middle of the garden that God showed to Adam and Eve from which he told them that they must not eat.

God told Adam and Eve that this was the tree of knowledge and therefore eating the fruit from this tree was forbidden, as it would allow Adam and Eve to know about good and evil. God also told them that if they disobeyed him and ate from the tree of knowledge then they would have to leave the Garden of Eden and they would die.

God said to Adam and Eve that as long as they obeyed him and they did not eat the forbidden fruit, they could always remain in the Garden of Eden and have eternal life.

One day whilst Adam was out tilling the land, Satan came to Eve in the form of a serpent and told her that she should eat one of the fruit from the tree of knowledge. Satan told Eve that if she ate the fruit she would become wise, but God was deliberately keeping them away from the fruit because he did not want them to have knowledge.

Although Eve remembered what she had been told by God, Eve looked at the fruit and they all looked so perfect and delicious to her. So Eve picked an apple, and she bit the apple and nothing happened to her.

As soon as Adam came home, Eve told him what she had done and encouraged him to taste the apple telling him how delicious it was. Like Eve, although Adam knew that it was wrong, he also ate the apple.

Soon after Adam and Eve had eaten the apple, they realised that all this time they had been walking around unclothed and they felt embarrassed, so they found some fig leaves to cover themselves.

Later that day, God came to talk to Adam and Eve but they hid behind the trees, as they were ashamed to face God after what they had done. But God knew what had happened and was angry that they had disobeyed him and had eaten the forbidden fruit.

Adam began to blame Eve for giving him the fruit and Eve told God that it was the serpent that had persuaded her to eat it. But God was angry with all of them, including the serpent. God told Adam and Eve that they would have to be punished and that they would have to leave the beautiful Garden of Eden and go out in the world and fend for themselves.

God also punished the serpent by putting a curse on his kind. God said that all serpents and animals like him would become man's enemy and they would crawl on their bellies forever.

This story shows that God originally created humans to live in a paradise on Earth, but because Adam and Eve disobeyed God, instead humans have had to lead a life full of suffering and injustice. It also tells us that we should try not to give into temptation even when things look good, because this is likely to get us into trouble and change our lives in a way that is not good for us.

The Story of Cain and Abel

(Genesis 4:1-16)

After they had disobeyed God, and were forced to leave the Garden of Eden, Adam and Eve were very remorseful and asked God how they could be forgiven for what they had done. God told them that they could show him how sorry they were by sacrificing a lamb to Him.

Sometime later Adam and Eve had two sons. Their eldest son was called Cain and his younger brother was called Abel, both of whom grew up working with their parents helping them on the land.

Abel was a shepherd and helped them to look after the family's herd of sheep, whereas Cain was a farmer and he tended the land, growing vegetables and grain. Like most brothers, Cain and Abel loved each-other and generally got on but occasionally they fell out and had arguments.

One day Adam and Eve shared with their sons what God had asked them to do to show their commitment and appreciation to Him. So both Cane and Abel decided that they would make their own sacrifices to God.

Abel, who was a very hardworking and loving young man, thought long and hard about what he wanted to sacrifice to God and eventually decided that nothing but the best would do. So Abel chose his most prized possession, which was his best lamb and offered this to God.

Although Cain on the other hand wanted to please God, he was really taken aback that Abel had chosen his best lamb and mocked him saying that he's sure that God would have been just as pleased if he had received the 'runt' of the litter.

Cain decided that his own offering would be some left over straw that he no longer needed believing that God would not mind.

When God saw what the brothers had offered to Him, He was really pleased with Abel's offering, acknowledging that He had sacrificed his best lamb. However, He did not look favourably on Cain's offering and Cain saw this.

When Cain realised that the Lord had shown a preference for what his brother Abel had done, he became angry and struck by jealousy. God observed Cain and questioned why he was looking downcast and told Cain that if he had done the right thing like his brother he would not be feeling upset.

Cain however became even more incensed and decided to lure Abel out to the field by suggesting that they go for a walk together, and in a jealous rage he attacked and killed him.

When God saw what Cain had done, He asked him where his brother was. Cain responded, "I do not know. Am I my brother's keeper?"

God was angry and said to Cain that Abel's blood cries out to Him from the ground. God also told Cain that he would be cursed and that he would be driven from his family and become a 'restless wanderer' and that he would no longer be able to yield good crops from the soil.

Cain was immediately repentant for what he had done. Cain agreed with God in that he should be punished and become a restless wanderer, also stating that whoever finds him should kill him. However, God said that Cain would not be killed and that He put a mark on Cain, which meant that anyone who killed Cain would be punished 7 times over.

This story helps us to remember that we must always give our best to God and God will look favourably on us. It also shows that it is important not to allow envy to take over, as this could make us make bad and irreparable choices in our lives.

The Story of Noah and the Ark

(Genesis 6:1-22, 7:1-24, 8:1-21)

Many years after God had created mankind, he saw that man was no longer following his laws and that instead they had become corrupt and were living a life of wickedness and evil.

For instance, God saw that there was drunkenness, violence and men were also committing lots of crimes.

God was very unhappy, because He had created mankind in His own image so that they could obey His rules and lead a rich life of goodness and happiness. But instead He saw that man was living a life of corruption and sin and they were disobedient to His laws.

God also realised that wickedness had become a way of life to man and so they no longer walked in God's footsteps and they no longer feared Him. God was dismayed at the extent of man's behaviour and decided that in order to change things for the better He would have to destroy the world and start again.

God however, looked amongst His people and saw that a man called Noah had remained righteous and was still obedient to His law. God was very happy with Noah and His children and so He spoke to Noah and asked Him to speak to the people telling them to repent and change their ways, otherwise He would send a flood to destroy the earth. Noah did as he was told and went to the people asking them to follow God and ask for forgiveness for their sinful ways, as only this would prevent God from destroying the earth with a flood. The people mocked Noah and laughed at him. Some even tried to kill him!

When God saw how the people reacted to Noah, He told him to build a very large boat using very strong wood. God said that the boat would be called an Ark. God told Noah that He would be sending a flood to earth that would kill all mankind and most of the animals. God said that only those in the Ark would be saved.

Noah and his sons listened to God and they set about building a gigantic Ark with many rooms, which God had asked them to do. Noah made sure that they filled the Ark with sufficient food and water for them all and God was pleased. God sent two of every animal to go with Noah and his children on the Ark and as soon as the Ark was filled, God sent the rain to the land and the floods began.

It rained heavily every day non-stop for forty days and forty nights and the land was completely covered with water. All the people and the animals left on the land died except Noah, his family and all the animals that he had taken with him on the Ark, who all survived and were safe and sound.

Once the rain stopped Noah sent out a dove to check whether the land had once again become dry. When the dove did not return Noah and his family left the Ark and returned to the land. Noah was very thankful to God for saving their lives and he praised Him and built an altar to make sacrifices to show his gratitude.

God was pleased with Noah because he had listened to Him and obeyed His commands. God also promised that He would never again send floods to destroy the earth. God sent the symbol of the rainbow to show that He would keep His promise. A rainbow can now be seen every time there is a storm to help us to remember that God will always keep His promises.

The Tower of Babel

(Genesis 11:1-9)

Many years after the great flood, Noah's descendants had settled in an area of Babylon in a land named Shinar. Although the population was growing, everyone still only spoke one single language. Babylon was one of the most powerful regions at this time and the people were full of pride. They spoke amongst themselves thinking of ways to ensure that they could make a lasting 'name for themselves.'

They then decided to build their own city. This city they said would be built using baked bricks and tar for mortar instead of using the usual stone. However, to make the city really stand out they decided that in the middle of the city, they would also build an enormous tower that reaches to the heavens.

This high tower would not only exalt them like God himself, but it would also stand out as a symbol of how great a nation they had become so that they would no longer need to follow God's laws to get to heaven.

The Babylonians, as these people were called, soon began to construct their great tower.

God looked down at the Babylonians and was not happy with what they were doing. God also did not like the pride and arrogance that He saw in the hearts of these people. God realised that if just by speaking the same language the people can do what they are doing, then this could also mean that they could make plans which may be even worse.

For this reason God decided that He would confuse their languages so that they could no longer be able to communicate freely to each other, and they would not be able to understand one another.

All of a sudden everyone began to speak different languages so they could not talk to each other and neither could they work together to continue building the tower; the work on the tower had to cease and was left incomplete.

Because they could not communicate, this also caused everyone to leave the city and to scatter across the land, spreading the people far across the face of the earth. The remains of the tower were named 'The Tower of Babel' because the word Babel means confusion.

This story helps us to remember that we cannot build a successful life without God. It is also a powerful reminder of how important it is to keep obeying God even when we believe that we have everything we need.

The Story of Abraham and Sarah

(Genesis 12 -21)

There was once a man called Abraham who was married to a woman named Sarah. Abraham and Sarah were good people, but Abraham's wife was barren so could not have children.

One day God came and spoke to Abraham. He told him to leave his father's house and the country, telling him that he will lead him to a great new promised land where he and his family will be blessed and Abraham's name will be also be great.

Although he was already 75 years old, Abraham did as God had requested and he left his home, taking both his wife Sarah and nephew, Lot, together with all their belongings heading to the land of Canaan. Throughout their travels, Abraham would build an altar so that he could speak to God. God protected Abraham and his family and even though there was a famine, they continued to be blessed.

Whilst travelling through Egypt Abraham and his family amassed great wealth consisting of: cattle, gold, silver, menservants, maidservants and camels. Abraham continued calling upon the Lord, building an altar wherever he went. God was pleased with Abraham and told him that he would give him and his generations that followed all the land that they could see with their eyes.

When Abraham was aged 99 years, he was visited by 3 men. On seeing the visitors Abraham ran towards them offering food, drink and rest, ensuring that his wife prepared a good meal for the visitors. At that time God again came to Abraham and told him that within a year his wife Sarah would give birth to a son who would follow God's commandments. Sarah had however been listening behind the door of the tent and laughed because she could not believe that she would have a child at her age, as she was 90 years old. The Lord responded by saying, "is anything too hard for the Lord?"

Just as God had promised, despite her old age, Sarah conceived and gave birth to their son Isaac. Both Abraham and Sarah were grateful and continued to thank God for blessing them with a child.

This story shows that when we listen and obey God, what seems impossible becomes possible.

A Wife for Isaac

(Genesis 24:1-67)

After his wife Sarah died, Abraham wanted to find a wife for his treasured son Isaac, who was grieving his mother's death. Abraham called his most trusted servant and asked him to swear that he will never allow Abraham to marry a local Canaanite woman. Abraham told his servant to instead go to his original homeland, where his relatives still lived, to find Isaac a wife.

The servant was concerned that even if he found someone, that she would not want to travel the distance to Canaan, so he asked Abraham if he should instead take Isaac to live in his father's homeland. Abraham made the servant touch his right thigh and swear an oath that he would never take Isaac away from the land that was promised to Abraham's descendants by God.

Abraham told the servant that God will send an angel ahead of him to find a wife for Isaac. However, if she is unwilling to follow the servant back, then the servant will be freed from the oath.

The servant loaded ten of Abraham's camels with expensive gifts and set off for the town where Abraham's family had settled. The servant was faithful and prayed to God to give him success on his travel. As he approached the place, the servant made the camels kneel down by a well to rest. Here the servant asked God to show favour to his master and select, from one of the young women drawing water from the spring well, the woman who is willing to share her pitcher of water and allow both he and the camels to drink.

Soon afterwards, an attractive young woman called Rebekah, who was also a virgin and the granddaughter of Abraham's brother, arrived and filled her pitcher with water. When the servant asked her for some of her water, she agreed and also agreed that the camels should drink as well. The servant was very happy and he thanked Rebekah and gave her expensive gifts of gold earrings and two bracelets. He also asked Rebekah about her family and when he found out that she was related to Abraham, he bowed his head and praised the Lord, as he knew that this was God's doing and that God had led him to Rebekah.

The servant asked to meet with Rebekah's family and relayed to them what God had done. He also told them what Abraham had requested. Rebekah's parents agreed that this appeared to be what the Lord had intended, so they asked Rebekah if she was willing to go with the servant to become Isaac's wife and she agreed to go with their blessing. Before he left with Rebekah, the servant gave gifts of jewels, gold and silver to Rebekah's family.

As the servant was arriving with Rebekah and the camels, Isaac was also returning from his evening prayers in the field and so he came to meet them. The servant told Isaac about how he came to find Rebekah and Isaac immediately loved her and took her for his wife.

This story reminds us of the great rewards we get when we love and trust in God. As just as God's allowed Abraham's servant to find the perfect wife for Isaac, so too will God answer our prayers if we have enduring faith and continue to serve him.

The Story of Jacob
(Genesis 25:20-34)

When Abraham and Sarah's son Isaac was around 40 years old, he married Rebekah, who was the daughter of Bethuel the Aramean, from Paddan Aram.

Isaac prayed to God that Rebekah would have a child as she was barren and the Lord blessed her and she became pregnant with twins. Whilst pregnant Rebekah asked the Lord why the babies appeared to be fighting in her womb and He told her that she had two nations in her womb. God said that the two would become divided and that one would be stronger than the other and the older one would serve the younger. Thus, the young twin Jacob's life began with a struggle; as a twin in the womb with Esau he jostled for position and was born grasping his brother's heel however, Jacob's name is translated as 'he deceives'.

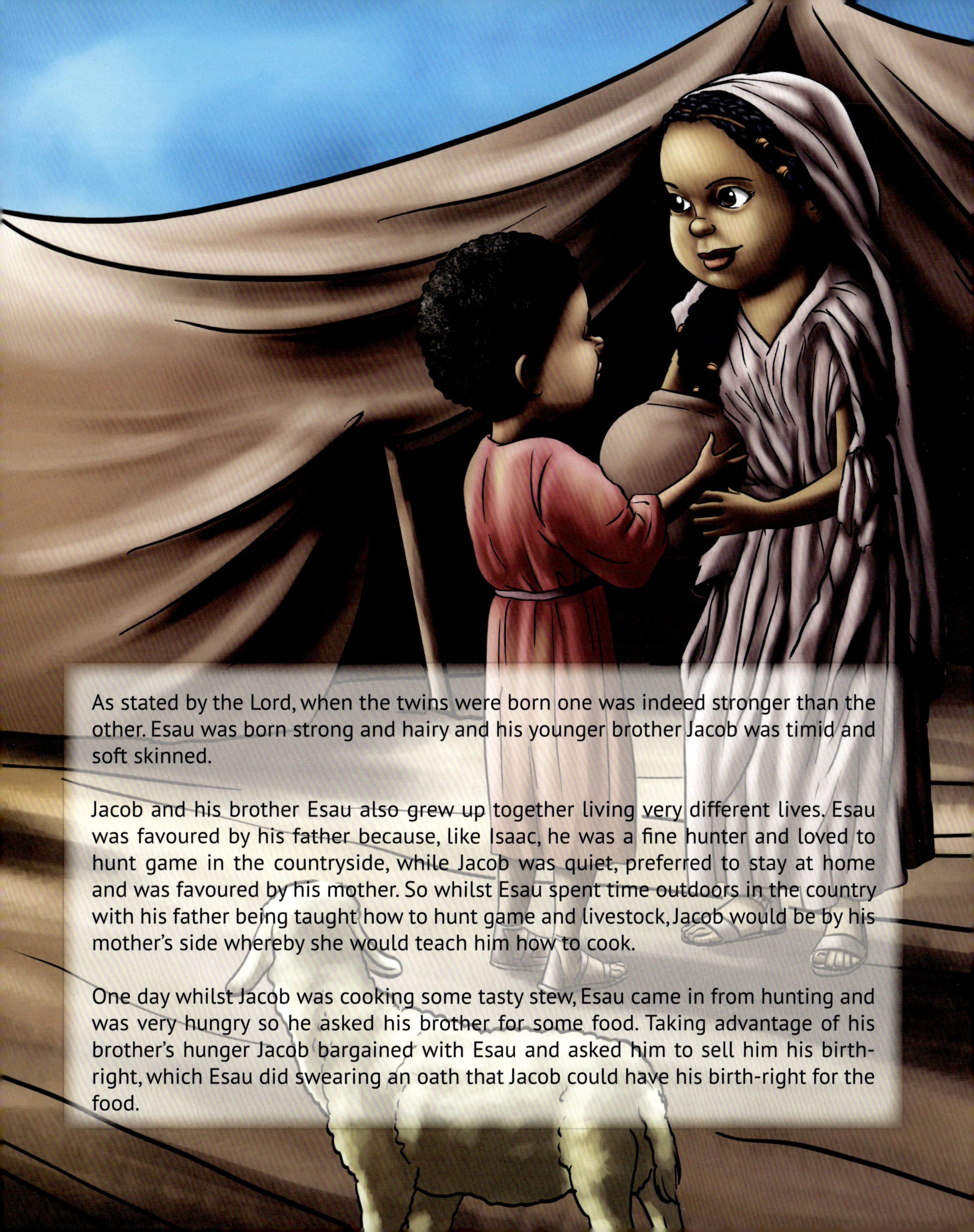

As stated by the Lord, when the twins were born one was indeed stronger than the other. Esau was born strong and hairy and his younger brother Jacob was timid and soft skinned.

Jacob and his brother Esau also grew up together living very different lives. Esau was favoured by his father because, like Isaac, he was a fine hunter and loved to hunt game in the countryside, while Jacob was quiet, preferred to stay at home and was favoured by his mother. So whilst Esau spent time outdoors in the country with his father being taught how to hunt game and livestock, Jacob would be by his mother's side whereby she would teach him how to cook.

One day whilst Jacob was cooking some tasty stew, Esau came in from hunting and was very hungry so he asked his brother for some food. Taking advantage of his brother's hunger Jacob bargained with Esau and asked him to sell him his birth-right, which Esau did swearing an oath that Jacob could have his birth-right for the food.

Jacob receives his Father's Blessing

(Genesis 27, 28:1-19)

When Isaac was old and his eyesight faded, he realized that he was near to his death and called his son Esau telling him that he wanted to bless him before he died as he was the firstborn son. On hearing this, Rebekah devised a plan to trick Isaac into blessing Jacob instead. Isaac had asked Esau to go out and hunt game and then to prepare a tasty meal for his father.

However, Rebekah told Jacob to quickly go and choose their best goats and bring it to her so that she could cook this for Isaac. Jacob obeyed his mother and brought the food that his mother cooked to his father. Isaac was surprised at how quickly his son had managed to get the food and asked Jacob to allow him to touch him to be sure that he was Esau. Rebekah had prepared Jacob for this and had covered his arms with goat's hair thus tricking Isaac into believing that he was Esau. Isaac also asked Jacob if he was really Esau and Jacob stated that he was. Isaac blessed him with abundance with the earth's richness, and stated that nations and people will serve him and that he would become Lord over his brothers.

When Esau realised that Jacob had received his father's blessing instead of him he was angry, especially as Esau remembered that this was the second time that he had been deceived by his brother. Esau vowed that once his father died he would kill Jacob as soon as the period of mourning for his father's death was over.

To protect her youngest son, Rebekah warned Jacob of his brother's vow, and goes to her husband and convinces him that Jacob should leave their home to try to find himself a wife from among her own family in Haran. Isaac agreed with his wife and Jacob is sent off to his uncle Laban who lived in their ancestral home of Haran.

During Jacob's journey, he has a dream of a ladder to heaven with God at the top and angels ascending and descending. This imagery is mirrored in Jesus' words to His disciple Nathanael. God gives Jacob His assurance of His presence and the fulfilment of His promise to Abraham. Because of this experience, Jacob renames the place 'Bethel', meaning 'house of God', and he makes a vow to serve God.

The story of Jacob shows how favouritism can be destructive and cause great resentment amongst siblings, which almost led to the loss of Jacob's life.

Jacob and his Two Wives

(Genesis 29:1-30)

Soon after Jacob arrives in Haran, he meets some shepherds who know of his uncle Laban and they introduce him to Laban's daughter Rachel who was also a shepherdess. Rachel immediately sends word to her father about his sister's son's arrival and Jacob is welcomed with open arms into his uncle Laban's home who tells him that he is welcome to stay as he is his own 'flesh and blood'.

After Jacob had stayed with Laban for a month, his uncle offers to pay him for the work he had been doing as a shepherd looking after his flocks. Acknowledging that he had fallen for Laban's daughter Rachel, Jacob agrees to work for seven years in return for Rachel, whom he loved deeply. However, at the end of the seven years Laban deceived Jacob and on Jacob's wedding night, Laban substitutes his older daughter Leah, who was not as beautiful as her younger sister, for Rachel.

The next day when Jacob questions Laban about his deception, Laban tells him that it is customary to marry the eldest daughter first. Laban persuades Jacob to agree to work for him another seven years if he wanted to marry his younger daughter Rachel. A week after marrying Leah, Jacob was allowed to marry Rachel which he did because he loved Rachel more than he loved Leah (vs. 30).

Leah was very fertile and gave birth to Jacob's firstborn son Reuben and she also had several more sons while Rachel remained barren and without child. Rachel was unhappy about not having any children and pleaded to Jacob to give her children, but Jacob told her that it was only God's will to allow her to give him a son not his. Rachel allowed her maidservant to be with Jacob and the maidservant became pregnant twice for Jacob and bore him two sons. Leah's maidservant also had two sons for Jacob. After Leah gave birth to a sixth son and God also blessed Rachel and she became pregnant giving birth to a son named Joseph.

In total his two wives and their maidservants gave Jacob 12 sons, and Jacob's sons would be the ancestors of the 12 tribes of Israel.

Jacob Flees from Laban and Prepares to Meet His Brother Esau

(Genesis 31, 32, 33:1-4)

After Rachel gave birth to his youngest son, Jacob decided that it was now time to return to his father's land having stayed tending for his uncle Laban's flock for almost twenty years. Laban begged him not to leave and then promises Jacob that he will let him have all the speckled or spotted sheep as payment for all the work that he has done for him. However, before Jacob could separate the sheep, Laban himself removed all the speckled male and female goats and gave them to his own sons. Despite this Jacob continued to tend to the remaining flock, who not only began to give birth to flecked and spotted lambs, but they were also strong which enabled Jacob to set them apart from the others, many of whom were very weak.

Eventually, Jacob began to hear rumours that Laban's sons were saying that he had taken everything from their father and that even Laban himself had changed his attitude towards Jacob.

At that time God commanded Jacob to return to the land of his fathers accompanied by God's promise "And I will be with you." So, without telling Laban, Jacob leaves Haran, taking with him his wives and children and all the vast flocks that he had accumulated. However before they had left, without Jacob's knowledge his wife Rachel had also taken some of her father's idols with them.

As soon as Laban learnt that Jacob had left, he set off in hot pursuit especially as he had discovered that his idols had been stolen. Laban caught up with Jacob after seven days however Rachel managed to conceal the idols from her father during his search. Laban and Jacob eventually part company after swearing an oath not to invade each other's lands or to harm any of its inhabitants. Laban embraced his daughters and his grandchildren goodbye and returned home.

Jacob continued his journey home and though twenty years had passed since they had last seen each other he had not forgotten that his brother Esau had pledged to kill him and so he sent word ahead to tell Esau that his servant Jacob has plenty cattle, sheep and goats and is now returning home to find favour in his brother's eyes. Jacob also divided his cattle into two groups sending messengers ahead of him with gifts instructing them to tell Esau that he is following on. That night, Jacob experiences the greatest challenge of his life when he wrestles all night with a man whom he later learns is God. During the wrestling Jacob is blessed by God and given the promised new name of "Israel," the name that would remain with his descendants and be the name of the land that they were promised by God until the present day.

To Jacob's relief, when he finally meets his brother the reunion with Esau is a warm and welcoming one as Esau came out to meet him with his arms open wide.

This story reminds us that God remained faithful to Jacob despite Jacob's faults, and that God chose him to be the leader of a great nation that still bears his name today. We should therefore consider the life of Jacob and know that, when we are in times of trouble and fearful of the outcome, like Jacob we should humbly call on God and remind Him of His promises to us, and as with Jacob, God will fulfil his promises and that also in spite of our failings, God can and will still use us in His plan.

The Story of Joseph

(Genesis 37)

Out of all the sons that Jacob (who was also called Israel) had, his youngest son Joseph was his favourite and all his brothers hated him for this. Jacob even gave Joseph a richly decorated robe that made Joseph stand out and his brothers disliked him even more.

One day Joseph told his brothers about a dream that he had where he dreamt that they were all binding sheaves of corn in the fields when suddenly his sheaf rose and stood upright whereas his brothers' sheaves seemed to gather around his sheaf as if to bow down to it. Joseph's brothers said to him 'What is this dream? Do you intend to reign over us and actually rule us? And they began to despise him more.
However Joseph shared yet another dream with his brothers but this time he also told his father what he had dreamt. Joseph said that in his dream the sun, the moon and eleven stars were all bowing down to him. Jacob questioned Joseph about his dream asking whether he believes that both his parents and his brothers will actually come and bow down to the ground before him. This dream again made his brothers further jealous and although Israel was not happy about what he had heard, he pondered on the dream wondering what it could mean?

One day Israel called Joseph to him and told him that he wanted him to go and check on his brothers who were tending to their father's flock of sheep near the land of Shechem to make sure that all was well.
Joseph did as his father asked and went off in search of his brothers. However when he arrived at Shechem, his brothers were not there. Whilst there a man saw Joseph wandering the fields and he asked him what he was looking for? Joseph explained to the man that he was looking for his brothers who he expected to find grazing their flocks.
The man told Joseph that his brothers had moved on and that he had heard them say that they were going to a place called Dothan.

Joseph therefore set off for the land of Dothan to find his brothers.
However his brothers saw him coming from a distance and because of their hatred for him they all plotted to kill him.
"Here comes that dreamer" they said," let's throw him into one of the wells and say that he was killed by a ferocious animal."

When Reuben heard what they had planned, he wanted to protect his brother and hopefully bring him back to his father, so he urged them not shed Joseph's blood, but instead to simply throw him in the cistern and leave him in the desert.

When Joseph arrived where his brothers were with the flock, they stripped him of his fancy robe and threw him into the well, which was dry and didn't have any water and they left him there whilst they sat down to eat.

Shortly after Joseph's brothers had thrown him into the well, they saw a caravan of Ishmalites approaching from Gilead. They also saw that the Ishmalites' camels were loaded with spices, balm and myrrh, which they intended to sell in Egypt. So Judah said to his brothers 'Why kill our brother and have blood on our hands, what will we gain? Come let us sell him to the Ishmalites as after all he is our brother and so they all agreed to do this.
The brothers sold Joseph to the Ishmalite merchants for 20 pieces of silver and the Ishmalites took Joseph with them to Egypt.

When Reuben came back from tending his sheep and looked in the well, and saw

that Joseph was not there, he was upset and tore at his clothes in sorrow. He then went to his brothers and said "The boy is gone what am I going to do?"

The brothers then killed a goat and dipped Joseph's ornate coat in the blood of the goat and took it to their father telling him that they had found the coat and wanted him to examine the coat to see if it belonged to Joseph.
On seeing the coat covered in blood, Jacob immediately recognized it as Joseph's and said "Some ferocious animal has devoured my son and torn him to pieces. Jacob was so devastated that he put on a sackcloth and went into mourning and refused to be comforted by any of his remaining children.

Meanwhile when the Ishmalites arrived in Egypt the merchants sold Joseph to a man called Potiphar who was one of the Pharaoh's officials and was the captain of the guards.

Whilst he was living with his master Potiphar, the Lord blessed Joseph and made him prosperous in everything that he did. Potiphar observed that Joseph was favoured by the Lord and so he made him his attendant and entrusted into Joseph's care everything that he owned including putting him in charge of his household.

This story shows how Joseph's brothers plotted to kill him simply because Joseph was favoured by his father amongst his brothers and this caused his brothers to become envious. The situation became worse when Joseph perhaps arrogantly reported his dreams showing that his brothers and father would all bow down to him even though he was the youngest in the family. However God will never allow our enemies to win and He will continue to bless us even when it appears that our life is not going according to how we expected it be.

Joseph Interprets Pharoah's Dreams

(Genesis: 39:1-23, 41:1-56, 42 -44)

With Joseph now in charge, the Lord extended his Blessings to everything that Potiphar had both in his household and in the fields.
Sadly Potiphar's wife who was attracted to Joseph told lies on Joseph because he rejected her, telling her husband that Joseph had tried to make advances towards her and because he believed his wife, Joseph was thrown into prison.

The Lord continued to bless Joseph whilst he was in prison allowing him to find favour with the prison guards who put Joseph in charge of his fellow prisoners. The Lord even enabled Joseph to interpret complex dreams and news of this reached Pharaoh who himself had been seeking someone to interpret two dreams that had been troubling him. Pharaoh sent for Joseph and Joseph told him that it is God that will interpret his dreams, not him.

Joseph told Pharaoh that the dreams showed that the land of Egypt will have seven years of plentiful abundance followed by seven years of extreme famine. Joseph said that Pharaoh would need to find a wise man to ensure that during the years of plentiful, commissioners were appointed to collect and store up a fifth of all the harvest to be held in reserve for the country of Egypt.

Pharaoh was so pleased with the plan that he heard that he said to Joseph. 'Since God has disclosed this to you, there is no one as discerning and wise as you.' Pharaoh then appointed Joseph to be second in command and to be in charge of his palace. Pharaoh dressed Joseph in fine robes, put a gold chain around his neck and also gave Joseph his signet ring from his own finger.

Just as Joseph had said, there was seven years of plentiful abundance and after this followed seven years of famine in all lands, but in the whole of Egypt there was food. When even the Egyptians began to cry out to Pharaoh for food, he sent them to Joseph who opened the storehouses and sold them grain that had been stored.

The famine was so bad that many other countries also came to Egypt to buy grain.

The story illustrates how God sometimes works through our dreams to communicate his plans for us and even if his plans mean that we may have to go through hard times, we must persevere and we will gain God's favour.

Joseph Reveals Himself to his Brothers

(Genesis 42-47)

Soon Jacob who was in Canaan had heard that there was grain in Egypt and he sent ten of his sons to Egypt to buy grain. However as he was fearful that harm might come to Joseph's brother Benjamin, he would not allow him to go with his brothers.

When his brothers arrived in Egypt and presented themselves to Jacob to buy grain, he immediately recognized them, but pretended that he didn't know who they were as they did not recognise him. Jacob asked them where they were from and when they said that they had come from Canaan, remembering his dreams many years ago, he accused them of being spies who were conspiring to see where Egypt was unprotected.
They responded 'No my lord, we are not spies, we are your servants, honest men, who have come to buy food.' But Joseph challenged them again telling them that he thought that they were spies. The brothers were scared and disclosed to Joseph their background how they were originally 12 brothers but one died and the youngest remained at home with their father as he feared losing him.

Joseph again accuses his brothers of being spies and throws his brothers into prison for three days. Eventually Joseph asks them to prove their honesty to him by them returning to Canaan with the grain, leaving their brother Simeon behind. Joseph tells them that they must bring back their youngest brother Benjamin to verify that they are telling the truth, so that he does not have to kill them.

Joseph sends his brothers back to their country whilst giving orders for the donkeys to be filled with provisions for their journey as well as grain and for their bags of silver to be returned to them.

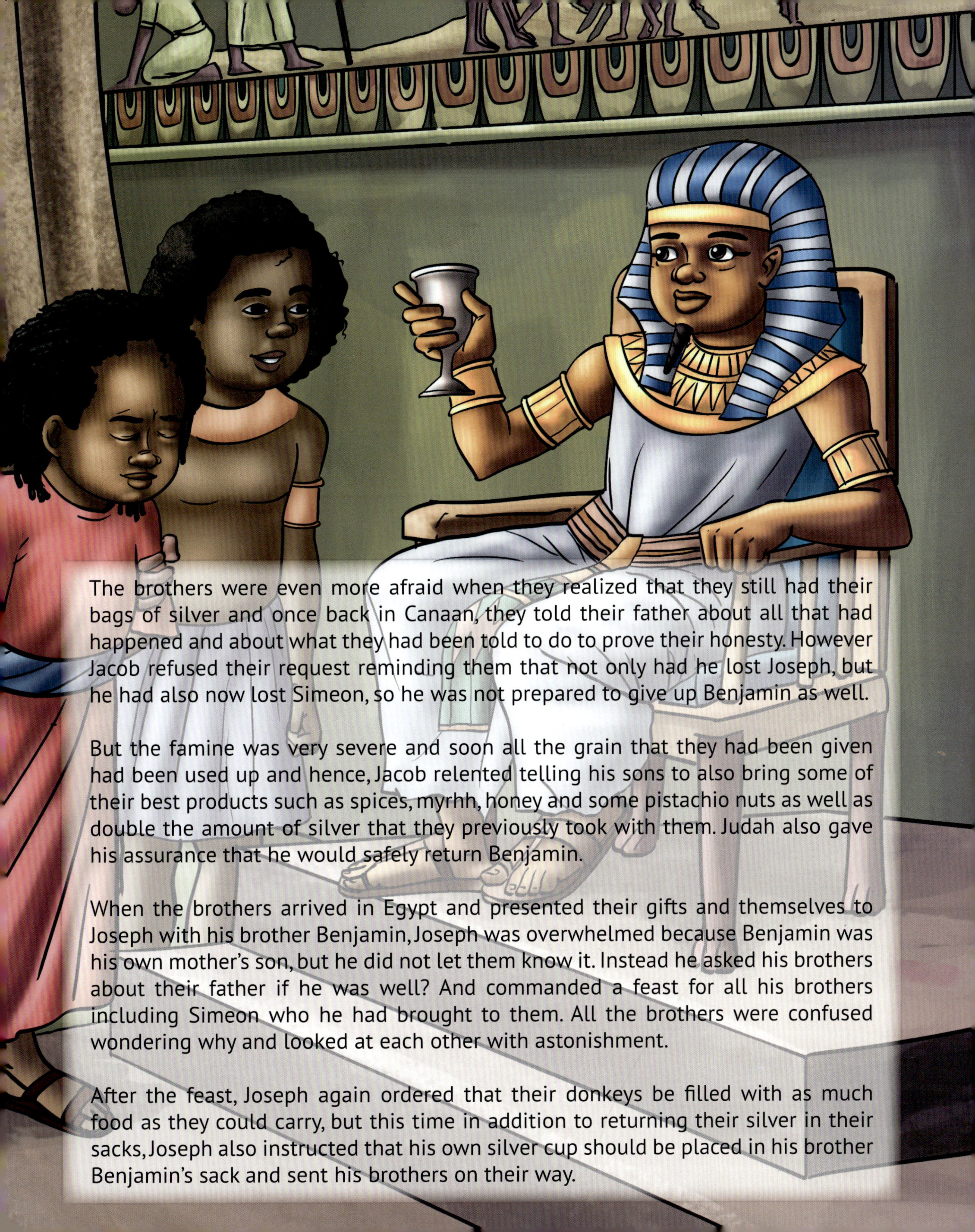

The brothers were even more afraid when they realized that they still had their bags of silver and once back in Canaan, they told their father about all that had happened and about what they had been told to do to prove their honesty. However Jacob refused their request reminding them that not only had he lost Joseph, but he had also now lost Simeon, so he was not prepared to give up Benjamin as well.

But the famine was very severe and soon all the grain that they had been given had been used up and hence, Jacob relented telling his sons to also bring some of their best products such as spices, myrhh, honey and some pistachio nuts as well as double the amount of silver that they previously took with them. Judah also gave his assurance that he would safely return Benjamin.

When the brothers arrived in Egypt and presented their gifts and themselves to Joseph with his brother Benjamin, Joseph was overwhelmed because Benjamin was his own mother's son, but he did not let them know it. Instead he asked his brothers about their father if he was well? And commanded a feast for all his brothers including Simeon who he had brought to them. All the brothers were confused wondering why and looked at each other with astonishment.

After the feast, Joseph again ordered that their donkeys be filled with as much food as they could carry, but this time in addition to returning their silver in their sacks, Joseph also instructed that his own silver cup should be placed in his brother Benjamin's sack and sent his brothers on their way.

A short time after they had left, Joseph sent one of his officials after them telling him to ask his brothers why they had decided to exchange good for evil by stealing Joseph's own silver cup. When the official caught up with the brothers, they denied any wrong doing and agreed that anyone who was found with the silver cup would become the Egyptian's slave.

The official began his search and the cup was finally found in Benjamin's sack. When they saw this, the brothers were distraught tearing at their clothes before humbly returning to the city of Egypt.

When the brothers arrived at Joseph's house, they threw their selves at Joseph's feet begging for a chance to prove their innocence, whilst agreeing to become Joseph's slaves because of what had been found in Benjamin's sack. And when Joseph told them that only Benjamin would become his slave, Judah begged Joseph to take him instead. Judah also shared what he agreed with his father telling Joseph that his father was elderly and could not bear the loss of his youngest son, especially after having already lost Benjamin's brother.

Eventually Joseph could no longer bear it, so he dismissed his attendants and called his brothers to him, throwing his arms around Benjamin, weeping and telling his brothers that he was their brother Joseph who they had thrown into the well and then sold to the Egyptian merchants. Joseph however told them not to be upset, as it was part of God's plan to send Joseph to Egypt ahead of the famine. Joseph also explained how he had become second in command to Pharaoh and was now a great and wealthy ruler in Egypt.

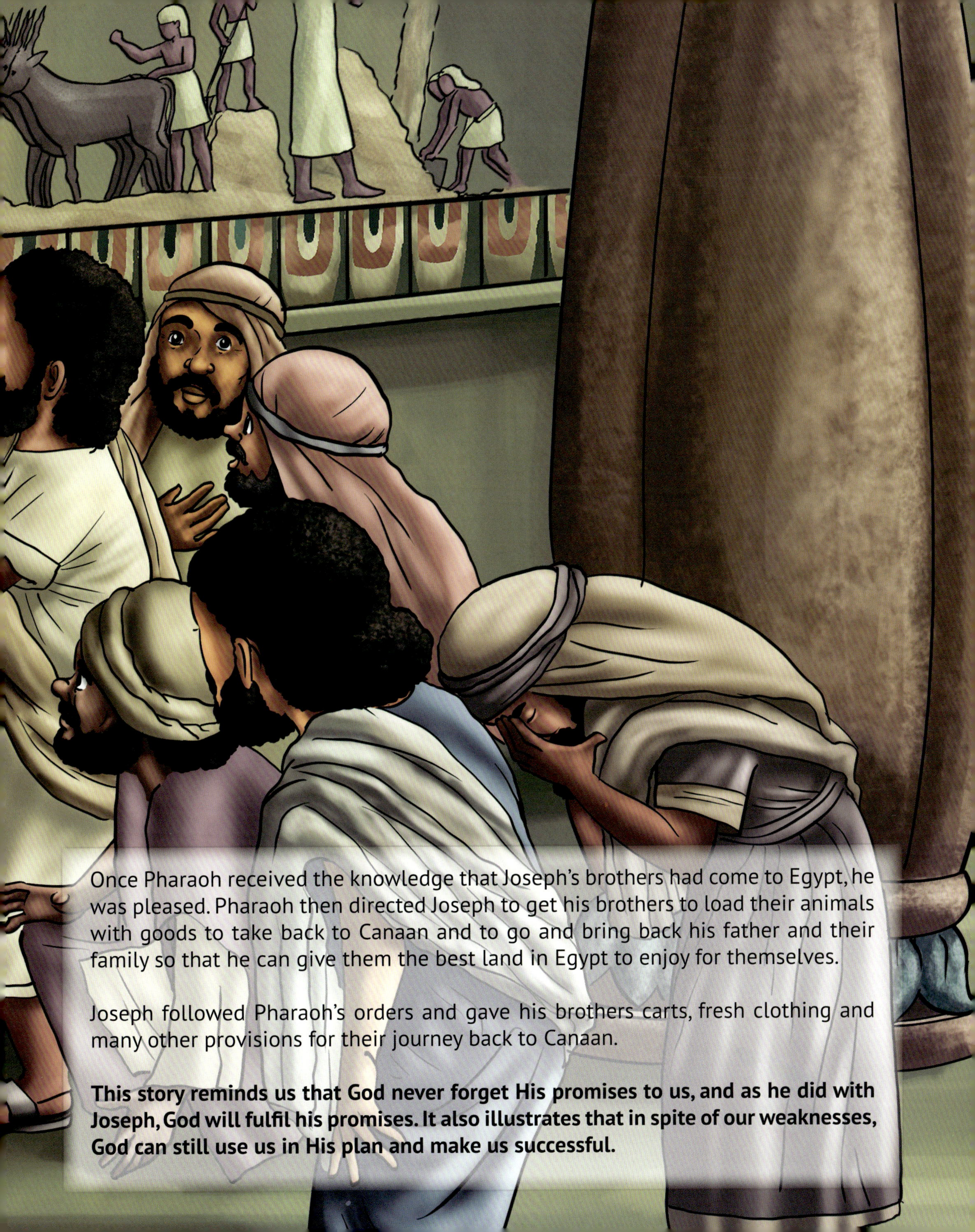

Once Pharaoh received the knowledge that Joseph's brothers had come to Egypt, he was pleased. Pharaoh then directed Joseph to get his brothers to load their animals with goods to take back to Canaan and to go and bring back his father and their family so that he can give them the best land in Egypt to enjoy for themselves.

Joseph followed Pharaoh's orders and gave his brothers carts, fresh clothing and many other provisions for their journey back to Canaan.

This story reminds us that God never forget His promises to us, and as he did with Joseph, God will fulfil his promises. It also illustrates that in spite of our weaknesses, God can still use us in His plan and make us successful.

The Story of Moses

(Exodus 2:1-10)

After the great famine, the Israelites lived in Egypt for a very long time, and had lots of children. The new Pharaoh did not like the Israelites and thought that there were too many of them. So, to stop them from becoming too strong and powerful, he made them work hard as slaves and treated them very badly.

Pharaoh eventually declared that all Israelite baby boys had to be killed, and sent out people to kill them. One mother managed to hide her baby boy for 3 months, and then when she could no longer hide him she placed him in a basket amongst the tall grass in the river. His sister stood and watched him.

Pharaoh's daughter was bathing in the river at the time and she found the baby in the basket crying and felt sorry for the baby. She wanted to take him home and be his mother, but she needed someone to help take care of him. The baby's sister saw what had happened and offered to find someone to help take care of the baby. She then ran back to her mother and her mother went with the Pharaoh's daughter to take care of the baby.

Pharaoh's daughter named the baby Moses and he lived with her in the Pharaoh's house, unknowingly being nursed by his own mother. However, when he was old enough Pharaoh's daughter adopted him as her own son.

Moses grew up and became a man. His people the Israelites were still slaves in Egypt and it saddened him to see them treated so badly.

One day, Moses saw an Egyptian beating an Israelite, this made Moses angry and he killed the Egyptian. The Pharaoh found out what Moses had done, so Moses had to run away to Midian where he lived as a Shepherd for many years.

This story shows us that even from his birth God had made plans to ensure that Moses would be kept safe from harm as He had great plans for Moses. Moses grew to be a compassionate man and although he lived in Pharaoh's house, he knew that he was not an Egyptian and was therefore troubled by how the Egyptians treated his fellow Israelites.

Moses, The Plagues & The Passover

(Exodus 2:1-10)

One day whilst Moses was looking after his sheep on Mount Horeb, he came across a burning bush that, although was alight, was not burning up.

The voice of God spoke to Moses from the bush and told him to lead the Israelites out of Egypt to the Promised Land, as he did not want to see his people suffer anymore.

Moses did not believe he would be able to do this, so God promised to help him.

First, he told Moses to throw down his staff and when he did, it turned into a snake, but when he picked it up it was a staff again.

Then he told Moses to put his hand inside his cloak. Moses did this and when he looked at his hand it was covered in disease. Moses put his hand back inside his cloak and when he looked again it was cured.

God told Moses to show these miracles to Pharaoh and he will free the Israelites.

Moses was still worried that he would not be able to convince the Pharaoh, so God told him that he could get his brother Aaron to help him.

Moses and Aaron went to see Pharaoh and told him that the God of the Israelites has said he must set his people free or bad things will happen: Pharaoh refused.

So, God turned the water in the Egyptian rivers into blood and none of the people could drink it and the fish began to die.

Again, Moses asked the Pharaoh to let the Israelites go, but still the Pharaoh refused. Then God filled all the Egyptian houses with frogs. There were frogs everywhere but still the Pharaoh refused to set the Israelites free.

Then God sent lice to cover the people and flies filled the sky. They were everywhere but still the Pharaoh would not let the Egyptians go.

Next, God killed all the animals in Egypt and covered all the Egyptian people in sores. Pharaoh still would not listen.

So, God sent a hail storm to crush the crops of Egypt and locusts to eat all the fruit

and green plants that remained. The Pharaoh still refused to let the Israelites go.

God then sent a darkness over Egypt for three days and the Egyptians couldn't see anything! But again, the Pharaoh would still not listen.

Finally, God told Moses that he would kill the firstborn son of every Egyptian, including the Pharaoh's oldest son, and the firstborn of all the animals.

God told Moses that every Israelite father should find a lamb that has nothing wrong with it, kill it, eat it and put its blood on their doors. This way God would know which houses to Passover so that the firstborn son inside would not die.

God called this 'The Passover' and told Moses that the Israelites should always remember it by having a Passover dinner every year to remember that God saved their children.

The Israelites obeyed God and the firstborn sons of all the Egyptians died, including the Pharaoh's son. Pharaoh finally listened and let the Israelites go.

God showed Moses the way to go, but when they were near to the Red Sea, Pharaoh changed his mind again and sent his army to chase after them.

Soon the Israelites saw the Egyptian army coming and the Israelites were afraid. God told Moses to raise his staff towards the Red Sea and as he did it, God sent a strong wind and parted the sea.

A dry path appeared in front of them and the Israelites walked right through the sea with walls of water on each side of them.

When they arrived safely on the other side God told Moses to stretch out his hand, and when he did the sea came crashing down and drowned the Egyptian army who had tried to follow the Israelites through the parted sea.

The Israelites were now free, they sang songs and danced as they gave thanks and praise to God for leading them out of Egypt.

This story showed how God looked after His chosen people even when they thought it was hopeless with the sea in front of them and the Egyptians behind them. God demonstrated that once the Israelites put their trust in Him He would not fail them and instead He protected them and led them to safety by opening the Red Sea to allow them to cross before closing it again when the Egyptians tried to follow.

The Ten Commandments

(Exodus19:1-25, 20:1-21)

After escaping from Egypt, the Israelites travelled through the wilderness for two months, where God fed them manna and gave them water to drink. After travelling through the wilderness, they camped at Mount Sinai.

God told Moses to tell the people that if they obey Him fully and keep his laws then they will be blessed above all nations and will be seen as His treasured possession. Moses did as he was asked, telling the elders what God had said and they agreed to obey the Lord.

God was pleased when Moses reported back to him and told Moses that in three days He will be coming to speak to Moses so that the people themselves can hear Him speaking and trust Moses, but God said that He will come in a dense cloud. He told Moses to warn the people not to climb or touch the mountain when God will be coming down Mount Sinai as whoever touches the mountain will be put to death.

On the third day, there was thunder and lightening and the mountain was covered with a thick smoke and fire as Moses led the people out of the camp to meet with God. The smoke billowed as if from a furnace, and the mountain shook violently as God came down to speak with Moses.

God gave Moses two stone tablets that had the Ten Commandments written down on them.

1. Do not worship any other gods before the Lord your God

2. Do not make any idols or false images to worship

3. Do not use the Lord's name in vain

4. Remember the Sabbath day and treat it as holy, work for six days and rest on the Sabbath

5. Have respect for your Father and Mother so that you may have a long life

6. Do not kill or murder

7. Be loyal to your husband or wife and do not commit adultery

8. Do not steal

9. Do not tell any lies about people

10. Do not envy others or want what they have, whether this be a wife or husband, servant, donkey or anything that belongs to your neighbour

Because of the Ten Commandments, the people of Israel now knew how to obey God and to live a righteous life.

The Story of Moses teaches us that the one thing that God wants to do with each of us is to establish a close, intimate and personal relationship provided we obey His laws. Moses shows us that we must not be afraid to develop this kind of relationship where, if we surrender our life to God, God's purpose for us can be revealed.

The Golden Calf

(Exodus 32:1-35)

After God had spoken to Moses, Moses stayed on the mountain for forty days and forty nights and some of the Israelites became impatient waiting for him to return. They went to Moses' brother Aaron and asked him to make them an idol to worship as they did not want to worship God any longer as they had now lost their trust in Moses.

Aaron told all the men and women to bring him all their gold earrings, and when they did he melted the Gold earrings down and made an idol out of them that looked like a calf.

Aaron also built an altar near to the golden calf that some of the Israelites then used to make sacrifices on whilst they worshipped the calf.
The Lord God saw what was happening, and He was very angry at what He had seen His people do after He had brought them out of captivity from the Egyptians. He saw that despite this, they had now turned against Him and were worshipping false idols and so the Lord told Moses of His intentions to destroy the people for their wrong doing. Moses begged Him to show compassion to the people reminding Him of His promises to Abraham, Isaac and Israel to bless their descendants.

Moses then came down from the mountain with the two tablets with the Lord's Testimony written on them.

When Moses approached the camp, and saw the golden calf and some of the Israelites dancing around it, he became very angry and chastised his brother Aaron for their sins as he knew this was wrong and went against the Ten Commandments that God had given him.

Moses smashed the two stone tablets and threw the golden calf in the fire. He was upset with Aaron for helping the Israelites disobey God.

Not all of the Israelites disobeyed God, as there were some that didn't take part in worshipping the golden calf. Moses asked God for forgiveness and told them that they would be blessed but the others will surely die.

God told Moses to bring two new stones to the top of the mountain and when he did, God wrote the Ten Commandments on them again and gave them to Moses.

This story reminds us that we may come up against many people who might try to lead us away from God and use logic and reasoning to encourage us to reject God, in favour of false idols. Moses asked God for forgiveness and told the people that those who had remained faithful to God, would be blessed, whilst the others would surely die.

We should always try to follow God's laws and be accountable for our own actions if we want God to continue to bless us.

The Story of Gideon

(Judges 6-7:1- 25)

Many years had passed since Moses had led the Israelites out of Egypt, and since then they had not been very good in God's eyes. So once again, God was not happy with them, and instead of blessing them he allowed them to suffer at the hands of the Midianites for seven years.

The Midianites were cruel to the people of Israel and they would steal all their animals and eat or burn all their crops. The Israelites were fed up and didn't know what else to do, so they cried out to God asking him to help them once again.

Now even though God was not happy with the Israelites he still listened to their prayers and sent one of his angels to visit a man called Gideon.

Gideon had found a secret place where he could thresh wheat without the risk of it being taken by the Midianites, and it was here where the angel appeared to him. The angel told Gideon that the Lord God is with him and can see that he is a mighty and brave man.

Gideon didn't believe the angel and asked him if God is with him, why has he not helped the Israelites and performed great miracles like he had performed in the past to free them from the Midianites.

God answered Gideon and told him that he had chosen him because he was a mighty man and that it would be him that would save the Israelites from the Midianites.

Gideon was unsure if he would be able to take on such a task, as he was from a poor family and was the youngest of his father's children. But God told him not to worry as he would be with him and that they will defeat the Midianites as one army.

But Gideon still wasn't sure if he believed. So, he told God that he was going to place some wool on the ground, and if there was dew on the wool but not on the ground when he returned in the morning then he would know that God had chosen him to save the Israelites.

When Gideon returned the next morning the wool he left behind was full of water but the ground next to it was completely dry. But Gideon still wasn't convinced, so this time he said to God, "when I return tomorrow make the wool dry and the ground wet." Sure, enough when he returned the next day, the wool was dry and the ground was wet.

Gideon finally believed and called all the tribes together to be part of his army.

But God then told him he had far too many men, so he told Gideon to send home any of the men that were afraid. Twenty-two thousand men left and ten thousand men stayed.

God thought there were still too many men, so when they went down to the river to drink God told him to separate the men that lap up the water like dogs from the ones that kneel and drink from cupped hands. The men that drank the water like dogs were sent home, and only three hundred men remained.

With only three hundred men left in his army Gideon was quite scared, so God spoke to him in the night. He told him to take his servant down into the valley where the Midianites stay and to listen to what the Midianites were saying.

So, Gideon and his servant snuck down into the Midianites camp and listened carefully. Soon after he arrived he heard one of the Midianites telling his friend about a dream he had. The man said that he had dreamt a loaf of bread came rolling into their camp so fast that it struck a tent and made it fall over.

The friend told him that this was a sign of the sword of Gideon and that God had strengthened his hand and given him the camp of the Midianites. When Gideon heard this, he felt a lot better. He returned to his camp and divided the three hundred men into three groups, and gave them all trumpets and torches.

They Surrounded the Midianite camp and on Gideon's signal they blew their trumpets and yelled, "a sword for the Lord and for Gideon".

The Midianite army ran away crying as they fled, turning their swords against one another in all the chaos.

God had fulfilled his promise, and Gideon had led the Israelites into victory.

The story of Gideon, reminds us that when God calls us for a purpose, we must not be afraid, and instead we must trust in the Lord and that if we do, no matter whether we are from humble beginnings, we too can accomplish whatever mission God sets us and like Gideon, prove ourselves to be faithful, strong and mighty leaders of men.

The Story of Samson

(Judges 13-16)

The Israelites had disobeyed God once again so he allowed the Philistines to rule over them for forty, long years.

One day, an angel of God appeared to the wife of a man named Manoah. The angel told her that she would become pregnant with a special baby boy who will help to lead the Israelites to freedom.

The angel told her that her baby would need to make three promises to God.

1. Never to drink wine
2. Never touch dead things
3. Never to cut his hair

Soon after the woman became pregnant and had a son whom she called Samson. As Samson grew up he kept his promises to God and God blessed him and made him very strong.

Samson was so strong that one day he killed a lion. Immediately a swarm of bees came along and made honey in the dead lion's body. Samson decided to taste it, even though he knew it was breaking one of his promises to God.

Samson made up a very clever riddle about the lion and the bees: 'Out of the eater came something to eat, and out of the strong came something sweet'. No one could solve the riddle and this frustrated the Philistines so much. Eventually, Samson's wife who was also a Philistine, persuaded him to tell her the answer and when he did, she told all her friends.

This made Samson very angry, but he got even more upset when the Philistines gave away his wife to his best friend. By this point, Samson no longer liked the Philistines at all and the Philistines did not like Samson, and as time went on they did things to try and upset each other. However, Samson's strength continued to be the talk of the town.

Samson eventually met and fell in love with a woman called Delilah.

One day a group of Philistines visited Delilah and offered to pay her lots of money if she could find out the secret to Samson's strength.

Delilah asked Samson lots of times to tell her how he got to be so strong, but Samson would not tell her the truth. Then one day he gave in and told her that his strength was in his hair, and if it was cut, he would be as weak as any other man.

That night when Samson was sleeping Delilah told his secret to the Philistines and they came and cut his hair off. They took him prisoner and did lots of horrible things to him. They blinded him and made him work every day dragging a heavy stone wheel.

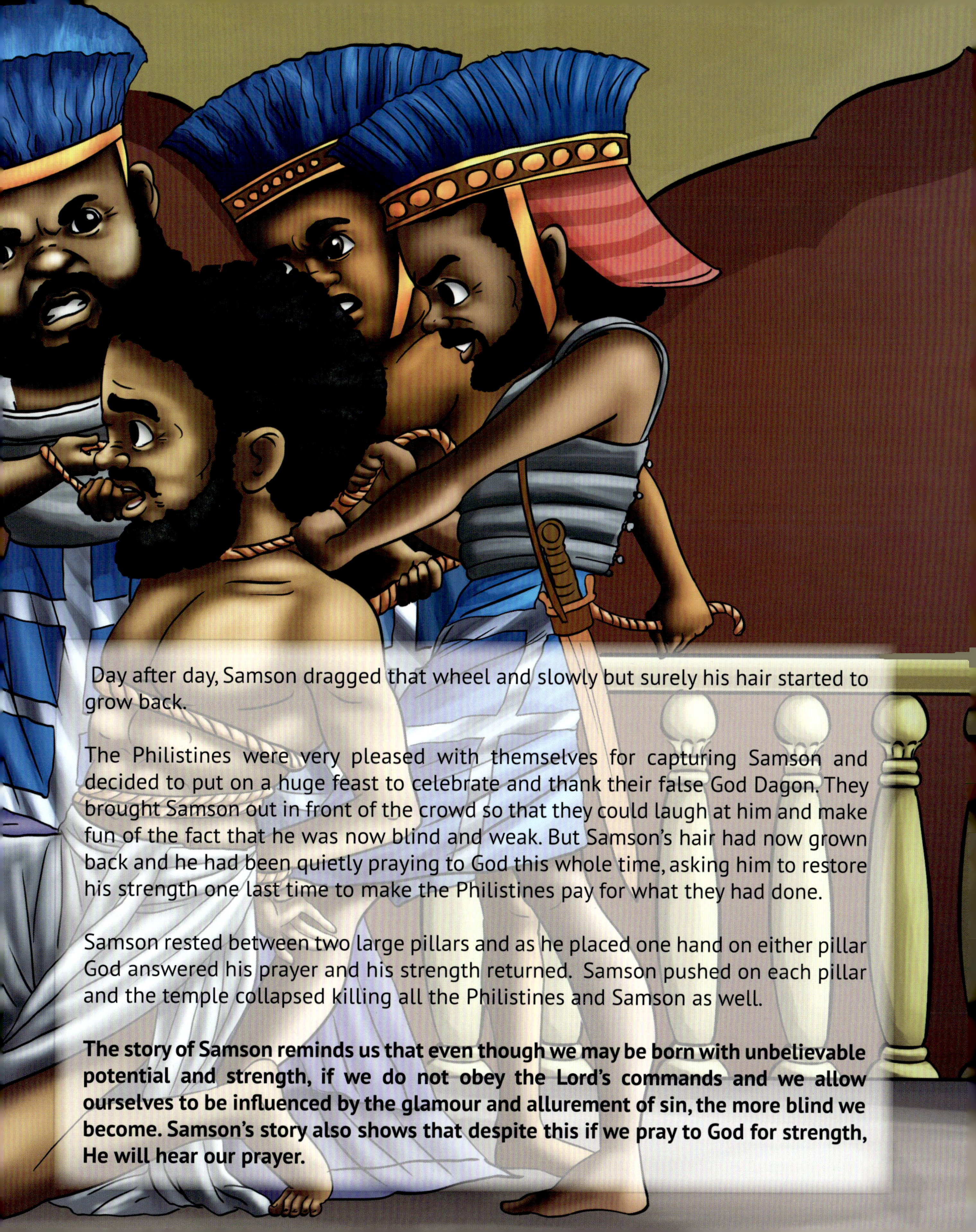

Day after day, Samson dragged that wheel and slowly but surely his hair started to grow back.

The Philistines were very pleased with themselves for capturing Samson and decided to put on a huge feast to celebrate and thank their false God Dagon. They brought Samson out in front of the crowd so that they could laugh at him and make fun of the fact that he was now blind and weak. But Samson's hair had now grown back and he had been quietly praying to God this whole time, asking him to restore his strength one last time to make the Philistines pay for what they had done.

Samson rested between two large pillars and as he placed one hand on either pillar God answered his prayer and his strength returned. Samson pushed on each pillar and the temple collapsed killing all the Philistines and Samson as well.

The story of Samson reminds us that even though we may be born with unbelievable potential and strength, if we do not obey the Lord's commands and we allow ourselves to be influenced by the glamour and allurement of sin, the more blind we become. Samson's story also shows that despite this if we pray to God for strength, He will hear our prayer.

The Story of Hannah's Baby Samuel

(1 Samuel 1-2:1-26)

There was once a man called Elkanah, who had two wives, one of who had many children and the other, Hannah, had none. Elkanah was a good man and every year he would go and make sacrifices to the Lord Almighty at Shiloh where the High Priest Eli had his temple.

Each year whilst making his sacrifices, Elkanah would serve portions of the meat to his children and both wives Peninnah and Hannah, but he would always give Hannah extra because he loved her and he felt saddened that she could not have any children.
Peninnah would always tease Hannah, which would make her cry and not eat although Elkanah told her not to be sad.

One year after they had eaten, Hannah wept and prayed silently and deeply from her heart to the Lord, asking Him to give her a son, vowing to never cut her son's hair and to let her son always serve the Lord if he lived.

Hannah was not aware that the High Priest Eli had observed her praying strongly, and because she had prayed silently at first, Eli thought that she was drunk and reprimanded her. However, Hannah explained that she was not drunk, but deeply troubled and that was why she was pouring out her soul to the Lord so that he could hear her prayer.

Eli told her to go in peace and said, "may the God of Israel grant you what you have asked him for." And Hannah no longer felt saddened.

When the family returned home, the Lord remembered Hannah and she conceived and gave birth to her son who she named Samuel, saying that she chose this name because she had asked the Lord to give her a son and he did.

Following Samuel's birth Hannah did not go with the family to make their annual sacrifices to the Lord. Instead, Hannah said to her husband Elkanah that as soon as their son Samuel was weaned, she will present him to the Lord and fulfil her vow to let him serve the Lord for the rest of his life.

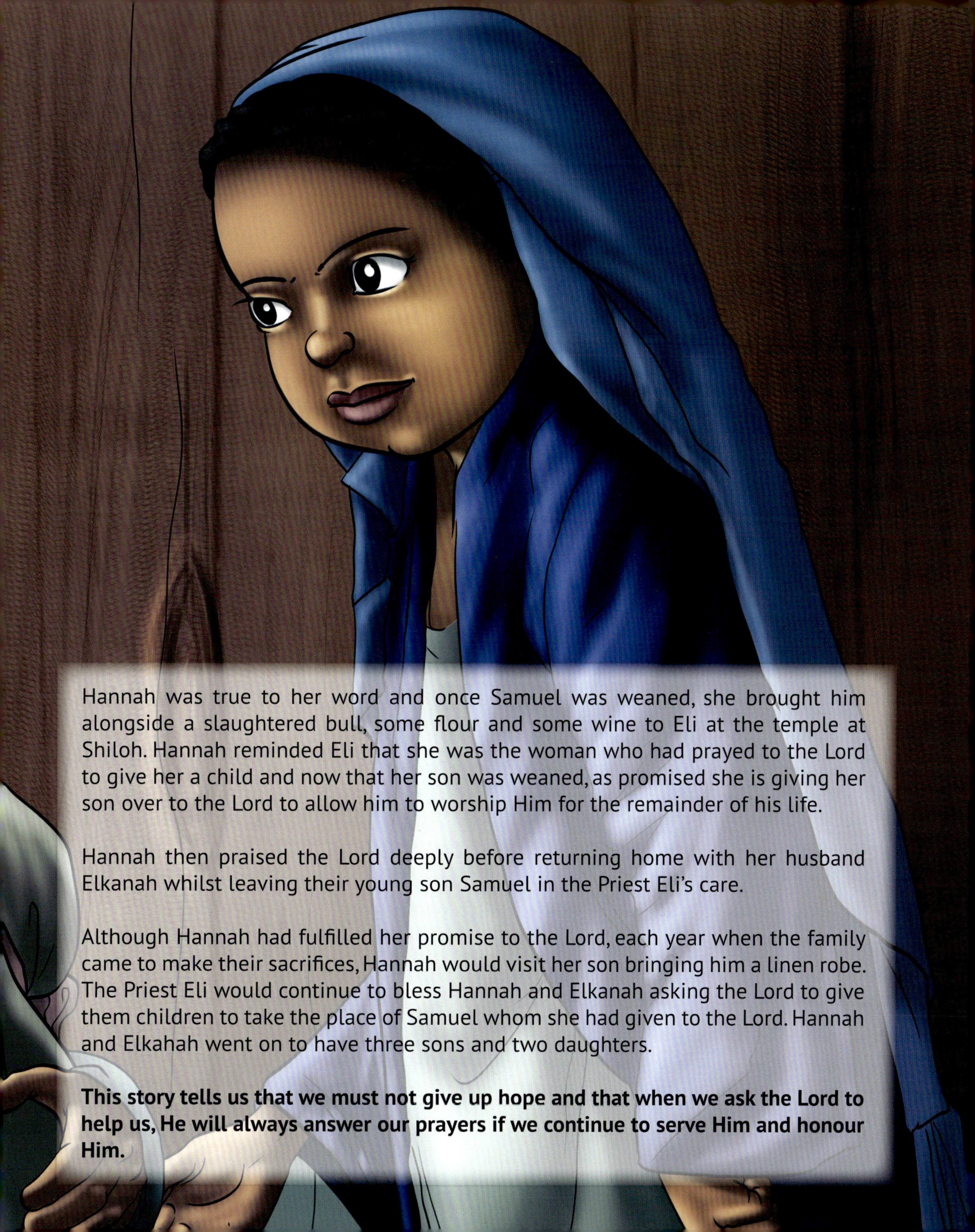

Hannah was true to her word and once Samuel was weaned, she brought him alongside a slaughtered bull, some flour and some wine to Eli at the temple at Shiloh. Hannah reminded Eli that she was the woman who had prayed to the Lord to give her a child and now that her son was weaned, as promised she is giving her son over to the Lord to allow him to worship Him for the remainder of his life.

Hannah then praised the Lord deeply before returning home with her husband Elkanah whilst leaving their young son Samuel in the Priest Eli's care.

Although Hannah had fulfilled her promise to the Lord, each year when the family came to make their sacrifices, Hannah would visit her son bringing him a linen robe. The Priest Eli would continue to bless Hannah and Elkanah asking the Lord to give them children to take the place of Samuel whom she had given to the Lord. Hannah and Elkahah went on to have three sons and two daughters.

This story tells us that we must not give up hope and that when we ask the Lord to help us, He will always answer our prayers if we continue to serve Him and honour Him.

Samuel Anoints Saul as King

(1 Samuel 9-10:1)

As Samuel grew older the Lord spoke with him and Samuel ministered before the Lord under his master, Priest Eli. Eli also realised that the Lord was with Samuel and that he continued to reveal Himself to Samuel through Samuel's words.
The Lord had told Samuel, when he was just a boy, that he would bring destruction on Eli's family because Eli had watched his sons Hophni and Phinehas show contempt during the making of sacrifices to the Lord, yet Samuel had done nothing to restrain them.

As ordained by the Lord, the people of Israel were defeated by the Philistines, who also captured the Ark of God, having killed Eli's two sons, Hophni and Phinehas. When Eli heard that the Ark of God had been captured and that his sons had both been killed, he fell down and because he was now a very old man he also died.

Although the people of Israel mourned the Ark of God, they continued to worship foreign gods. So Samuel urged them to commit themselves to the Lord and to serve him only and in this way he would deliver them out of the hands of the Philistines. The Israelites listened to Samuel who had become their leader and confessed their sins. Samuel then made sacrifices to the Lord and the Lord helped the Israelites to defeat the Philistines.

When Samuel grew old the people of Israel asked him to find them a king who would be able to lead them now that he had gotten old.

Samuel spoke to the Lord about what the people had asked for and the Lord was angry because once again the Israelites had rejected him. He asked Samuel to warn them solemnly about the perils that would befall them if they have a king to reign over them. He said that a king would take their crops and vineyards and use them as menservants and maidservants. However, as the people were adamant that they wanted a king, the Lord told Samuel to give them the king they wanted.

The Lord then revealed to Samuel that he will send a man from the land of Benjamin who Samuel must anoint as leader of the people of Israel. The next day a man called Saul arrived looking for the prophet who was Samuel. Samuel told Saul that it was he that Saul sought and invited Saul and his servant to eat with him telling Saul that the Lord had given him a message to give to him.

The next day, Samuel told Saul to send his servant on ahead and then Samuel took a flask of oil, pouring it on Saul's head and kissed him, saying that the Lord had anointed him leader over his inheritance.

This story reminds us that we do not need anyone other than God; it tells us that God really wanted Himself to be the Israelites' only ruler as He knew what was best for them and the dangers of having a human king. However, when the Israelites insisted on having things their own way, God gave them the king they asked for.

Samuel Anoints David as King

(1 Samuel 16: 1-23)

When Saul became the King of Israel he fought many long wars against the Philistines and many Israelites lost their lives. However, the Lord was not pleased with Saul because he disobeyed Him and did not follow His instructions. The Lord was grieved and told Samuel that because Saul did not follow his word, he will now reject Saul as King over Israel and will no longer bless him as he had previously done.

The Lord then sent Samuel to the house of a man called Jesse who lived in Bethlehem. The Lord told Samuel that He had chosen one of Jesse's sons to become the future King of Israel.

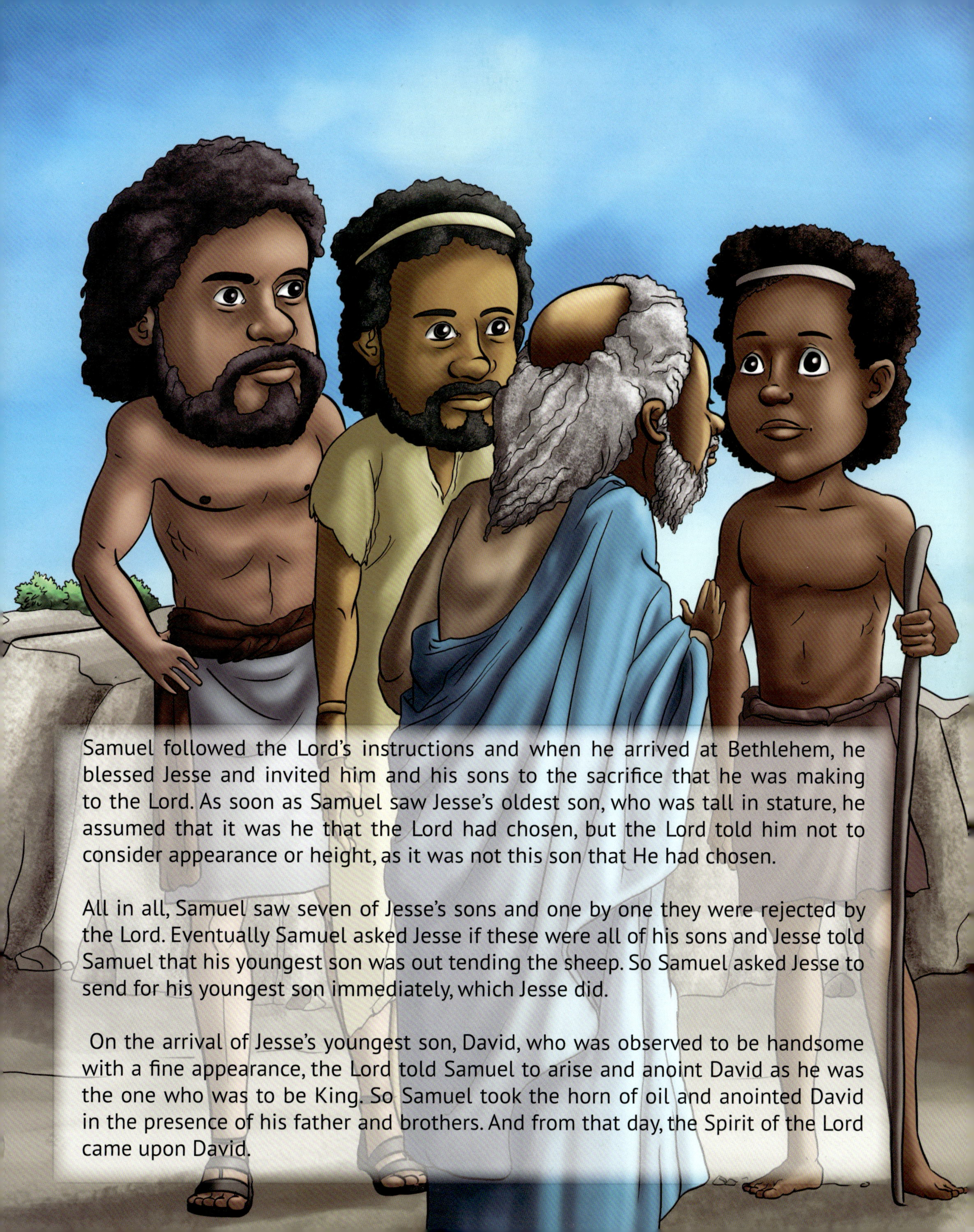

Samuel followed the Lord's instructions and when he arrived at Bethlehem, he blessed Jesse and invited him and his sons to the sacrifice that he was making to the Lord. As soon as Samuel saw Jesse's oldest son, who was tall in stature, he assumed that it was he that the Lord had chosen, but the Lord told him not to consider appearance or height, as it was not this son that He had chosen.

All in all, Samuel saw seven of Jesse's sons and one by one they were rejected by the Lord. Eventually Samuel asked Jesse if these were all of his sons and Jesse told Samuel that his youngest son was out tending the sheep. So Samuel asked Jesse to send for his youngest son immediately, which Jesse did.

On the arrival of Jesse's youngest son, David, who was observed to be handsome with a fine appearance, the Lord told Samuel to arise and anoint David as he was the one who was to be King. So Samuel took the horn of oil and anointed David in the presence of his father and brothers. And from that day, the Spirit of the Lord came upon David.

Once Saul had fallen out of favour with the Lord, he became tormented with evil spirits from which he could not find any relief.
It was known that whilst he tended to the sheep, David, the son of Jesse liked to play the harp and everyone who knew him was aware that he played the harp very well.

One day, after observing Saul being tormented by the evil spirits, Saul's attendants said to him that he should command his servants to search for someone who was able to play the harp, as this would soothe Saul and make him feel better. On hearing this, Saul immediately ordered his attendants to look for someone who could play the harp.

Pretty soon one of his servants told him about David, the son of Jesse, who lived in Bethlehem and who not only played the harp well, but was also a brave man. Saul sent word to Jesse, requesting that he send his son David to him. Jesse was honoured and sent David with gifts of bread, wine and a young goat.

On his arrival to the King, David was highly favoured by Saul so much so that he became one of his armour bearers. Saul also sent word to Jesse to ask if David could remain with him in his service, especially as when the evil spirit tormented Saul, David would play the harp and this would give Saul relief and the evil spirit would go away.

This story reminds us that although man looks at how someone appears on the outside, what God looks for is what He sees in a person's heart because God uses people who have a heart that will trust in Him.

David and the Giant Goliath

(1 Samuel 17: 1-58)

Whilst Saul was still the King of Israel, the battle between Israel and the Philistines continued. The Philistines occupied one hill whereas Saul and the Israelites occupied another and drew up battle lines for their respective camps.

Within the Philistine camp there was a champion called Goliath, who all the Israelites feared. Goliath was a giant of a man who was over nine feet tall, wore a bronze helmet and a heavy bronze coat of scale armour. He also wore bronze armour on his legs and had a bronze javelin type sword slung over his back. Goliath was fearless and came out every day challenging the Israelites to choose someone amongst them to come out and fight him. Goliath said that if the Israelites were able to send someone to fight him and kill him, then the Philistines would surrender to them, but if on the other hand, he was able to overcome and kill the Israelite then the `Israelites would become the subjects of the Philistines.

One day, Jesse called his son David and asked him to bring food to his older brothers who were on the battle line. Whilst there David saw Goliath and heard the Israelites saying that whoever defeats Goliath will be given great wealth from the King, and will also be given the King's daughter's hand in marriage and become exempt from paying taxes in Israel.

When Saul heard that David had been asking about Goliath, he sent for him. David told Saul that he would go and fight the Philistine but Saul replied, "how can you, who is still just a boy tending sheep, fight an experienced warrior?"

David told Saul that even as a shepherd he had fought off wild animals such as the lions and bears, who had tried to carry off his father's sheep. David said that the Lord who delivered him from harm when he fought off the lion and the bear, will also protect him and deliver him from harm from the Philistine.

When Saul heard David say this, he agreed telling David, "go and may the Lord be with you."

David even refused to wear the armour that Saul provided him with, stating that he wasn't used to wearing armour and this would hold him back. Instead he took with him in his pouch: a sling, five smooth stones from the stream and his shepherd's staff in his hand and went off towards Goliath.

When Goliath saw David and saw that he was just a boy, he mocked him. However, David was not deterred.

He said to Goliath, "you come to me with your sword, spear and javelin, yet I come against you in the name of the Lord Almighty, the God of Israel. This day the Lord will strike you down, cut off your head and I will give your remains and the remains of the Philistines to the birds and beasts of the earth."

As Goliath came towards David, David did not withdraw, instead he drew his sling from his pouch and took out one of his stones, which he then slung to strike Goliath right in the middle of his forehead. Goliath immediately fell face downwards onto the ground. So David ran and stood over Goliath and took the Philistine's own sword and cut off his head.

On seeing their hero dead, the Philistines turned and ran allowing the Israelite army to pursue and overcome them.

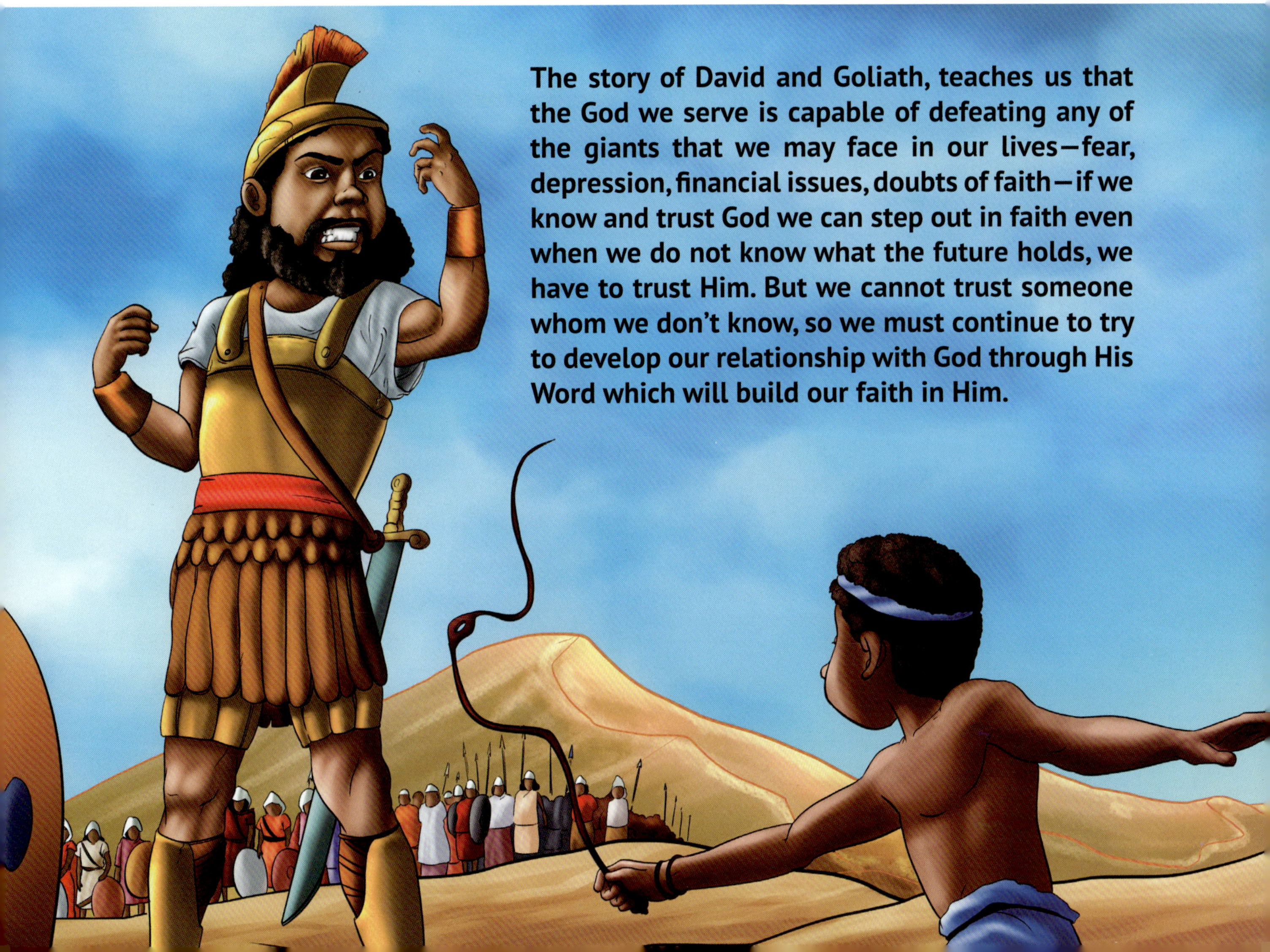

The story of David and Goliath, teaches us that the God we serve is capable of defeating any of the giants that we may face in our lives—fear, depression, financial issues, doubts of faith—if we know and trust God we can step out in faith even when we do not know what the future holds, we have to trust Him. But we cannot trust someone whom we don't know, so we must continue to try to develop our relationship with God through His Word which will build our faith in Him.

David Earns the hand of King's Saul's Daughter Micab

(1 Samuel 18 :1-28)

After David's triumph over Goliath, Saul kept him with him and did not let him return to his father's house. Whatever Saul sent David to do, he would carry out so successfully that Saul appointed him a high rank within the army. The people of Israel were very happy about this. So much so that when David returned home after battling the Philistines, the women came out to greet him singing songs of Joy; "Saul has slain thousands, and David tens of thousands."

Because the Lord was with David, he was very successful in everything that he did, leading his troops to victory in all their battles. Sadly, this angered Saul because he was jealous that he was no longer in the Lord's favour and this also made him afraid of David.
However, all the people in Israel and Judah loved David because of his great leadership in their campaigns. Saul's son Jonathan also loved David and they became good friends.

Because Saul had promised his daughter's hand to the person that killed Goliath, one day he came to David and offered to give his eldest daughter Merab to him in marriage, but only if he promised to serve him and continue to fight in his battles. In this way Saul had hoped that David would eventually be killed by the Philistines. David refused to take Merab, stating that he was from a humble family and was not worthy of becoming the King's son-in-law. So Merab was betrothed to another.

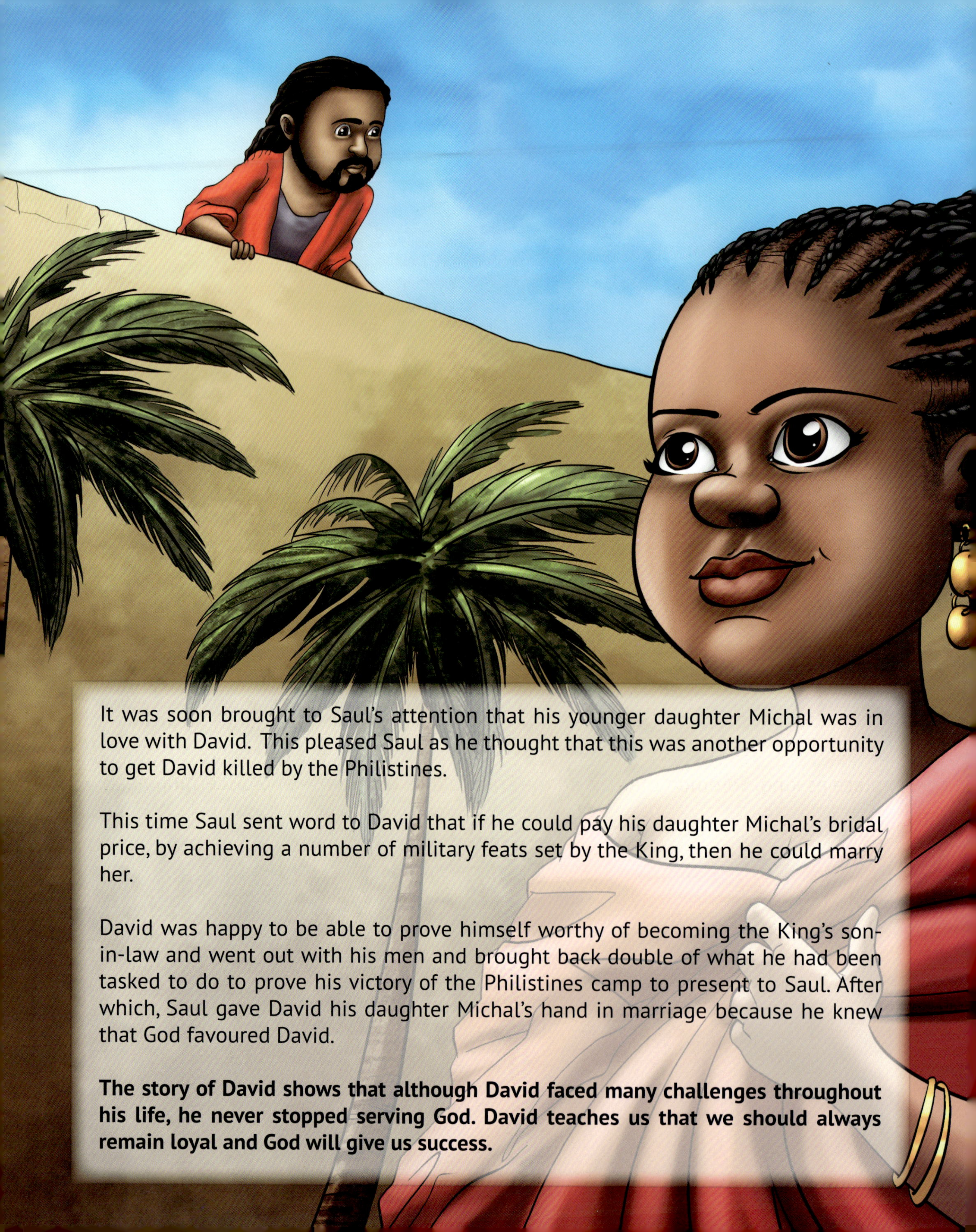

It was soon brought to Saul's attention that his younger daughter Michal was in love with David. This pleased Saul as he thought that this was another opportunity to get David killed by the Philistines.

This time Saul sent word to David that if he could pay his daughter Michal's bridal price, by achieving a number of military feats set by the King, then he could marry her.

David was happy to be able to prove himself worthy of becoming the King's son-in-law and went out with his men and brought back double of what he had been tasked to do to prove his victory of the Philistines camp to present to Saul. After which, Saul gave David his daughter Michal's hand in marriage because he knew that God favoured David.

The story of David shows that although David faced many challenges throughout his life, he never stopped serving God. David teaches us that we should always remain loyal and God will give us success.

The Story of Wise King Solomon

(1 Kings 2: 1-4,3:1-28)

David lived for a very long time and when it was almost time for him to die, he called his son Solomon to him and spoke with him. David asked Solomon to remain strong and observe the ways of the Lord.
David said,"walk in His ways and keep His decrees and commands, as written in the Laws of Moses, so that you may prosper wherever you may go."

After David gave Solomon much advice and guidance, David died and Solomon took his place on his father's throne and became the ruler of Israel.

Just like his father, Solomon was also blessed by the Lord. One day the Lord came to Solomon in his dream and God said to Solomon,"ask me for anything that you want me to give you."

Solomon firstly thanked the Lord for the great kindness that the Lord had continued to show both his father, David, and himself, and for allowing him to take his father's place as king. Solomon then asked the Lord to give him a wise and discerning heart to enable him to make good decisions as a king and to be able to know right from wrong.

Because the Lord was pleased that Solomon had asked for wisdom instead wealth or even for a long life, God said that He would not only grant him his wish, but He would also give him riches, honour and a long life.

One day, two promiscuous women came to King Solomon and stood before him with a baby seeking justice. One of the women told the king that both women lived in the same house and had given birth to sons a few days after each other. However, during the night when they were alone, the other woman's son had died because she had fell asleep on top of him and so the woman had swapped her dead baby for the baby that was alive.

The woman said when she awoke in the morning to nurse her son she saw that he was dead, but when she looked at him closely, she realised that the child in her bed was not hers. The two women then continued to tell Solomon that the child that was alive belonged to them.

The king said to both women, "you both say that the dead child does not belong to you and that this child is yours."

So, to settle the matter, the king asked for a sword, and gave an order for the living child to be cut into two halves and for each woman to be given half of the child. On hearing this, the woman who the child belonged to was filled with compassion and begged the king not to hurt her son. Whereas the other woman readily agreed for the baby to be cut into halves, stating, "neither of us shall have him."

When the king saw what happened, he ruled that the woman who showed compassion was the mother of the baby and that she should be given her child.

When the story of King Solomon's verdict became known to the people of Israel, they were amazed because they saw that the king had used God's wisdom in making his ruling.

This story shows how by listening to God and using the wisdom that he had been granted, Solomon was able to ensure that the baby was returned to his rightful mother. The story also tells us that we must turn to God and listen to him for advice when we may have to make difficult decisions, as the answer may not always be as straightforward as it seems.

Solomon and the Queen of Sheba

(1 Kings: 10:1-13)

Solomon's wisdom caused him to be well known and his fame spread to all the surrounding nations. Men came from far and wide to listen to Solomon, many of whom were sent by kings who had heard how wise Solomon was.

One day Solomon received a visit from the Queen of Sheba who had also heard about Solomon's fame and had now come for herself to meet this king whom she had heard so much about. The queen had brought with her on her travels to Jerusalem: camels with many spices, large quantities of gold and other precious jewels.

The Queen of Sheba also wanted to test King Solomon's wisdom and hence when she met with him, she asked him many hard questions all of which he was able to answer fully. None of the questions asked were too hard for the king to provide an explanation.

Having tested King Solomon with very hard questions and seen the abundance of good food, his many servants, his vast wealth and the great palace that he had built, the Queen of Sheba was overwhelmed.

Although she had heard reports of his fame and wisdom, she had not really believed that it was true and had not expected to be in awe of the king. The Queen of Sheba told King Solomon that her expectations had been far exceeded. She said, "how happy your men and your officials must be to be able to continually hear your wisdom."

The Queen of Sheba also praised God and acknowledged his presence in all that Solomon was doing, stating that because of God's eternal love for Israel, he had made Solomon king so that justice and righteousness could prevail in the land.

The Queen of Sheba gave the king large quantities of the spices, gold and precious stones that she had brought with her. In return, King Solomon gave the queen everything that she requested before she left and returned to her own country.

This story helps us to see how God will always bless us with wisdom, wealth and prosperity if we follow His laws and serve Him.

Solomon Builds a Temple

(1 Kings 6: 1-38)

When Solomon had been the King of Israel for four years, he decided to build a great temple in order to worship God. The reason for Solomon building the temple was because he had acknowledged that there was so much war and unrest between the lands whilst his father David was in power, that David could not build a temple. However, Solomon was thankful that throughout his own reign, God had brought much peace and harmony.
King Solomon also knew that it was God's plan for him to build a temple and the Lord had said this to his father before he died.

Solomon's temple however was like no other as it was magnificent in size and structure. This was because Solomon had made many preparations before building the temple and had worked peacefully with the neighbouring King Hiram so that he could use wood from the best cedar and pine trees within his land. In return, Solomon had ensured that Hiram was supplied with plenty of wheat to eat and olive oil.

The Lord saw what Solomon was doing and told him that provided he follows His laws and regulations and continue to obey Him, He will fulfil the promise that God gave to David, in that He will not abandon the Israelites.

Solomon used the best labourers, stonecutters and craftsmen from all over Israel ensuring that they were provided with high quality stone to make the foundations for the temple.

Solomon used gold to cover the whole interior of the temple, including the floor and the altar. He also prepared an inner sanctuary overlaid with pure gold within the temple where the ark of the covenant of the Lord could be set. Additionally, he extended gold chains at the front of the inner sanctuary and there were also beautiful cherubim carved on the walls alongside palm trees and flowers.

All in all the temple took eleven years to complete and when it was completed it was very impressive in all its detail and the Lord was pleased.

This story tells us that we must continue to worship God and obey His commands. Even when we think that God has answered all our prayers and given us everything we have asked for, we must continue to put Him first and He will not abandon us.

Solomon's Wives

(1 Kings 11:1-13)

Although Solomon was married to Pharaoh's daughter, he loved lots of other women and against God's wishes, he married many of these women from other foreign nations.

God was against Solomon marrying outside of his nation because he knew that these women did not follow his laws and instead they worshipped false gods and God knew that they would encourage Solomon to do the same. God had warned Solomon of this, yet he had not heeded God's wishes.

Just as God had predicted, as Solomon grew older, his wives began to lead him astray and turned his heart towards other gods so that he was no longer fully devoted to the Lord as his father had been.

When God saw that Solomon had not only begun to worship these gods, but even built altars for him and his foreign wives to worship their gods -burning incense and offering sacrifices to them- he became very angry.

God then told Solomon that as he had not done as he had been commanded to, as punishment He will tear down Solomon's kingdom and leave his ancestors with only one tribe to lead.

The Lord was angry because Solomon had turned his heart away from Him and was no longer keeping Israel's promise to obey God's command and to serve only God.

This story shows that we must always stay faithful to God. We must listen to his guidance, follow his commands and not allow others to lead us astray. As long as we do this, God will continue to bless us with goodness in our lives.

The Story of Elijah

(1 Kings 17:2-24)

Elijah lived during a time when Israel was ruled over by King Ahab. King Ahab, like many of the kings before him, was not loyal to God and encouraged the people of Israel to disobey God and to worship false Gods and idols.

King Ahab was married to the wicked and cruel Queen Jezebel. He built her a temple for the false God Baal who was supposed to be the God of weather who he and his wife worshipped.

God called upon Elijah to visit King Ahab to tell him that there will be no rain or dew in Israel until God declares it to rain.

After delivering the message, God led Elijah to a safe place by the river Jordan where there was a brook that he could drink water from and where God had commanded ravens to bring him food each day.

Elijah did as God commanded and so it was that the ravens brought him bread and flesh in the morning and evening, and he drank water from the brook.

After a while the brook dried up, as there had not been any rain and God spoke to Elijah again. This time telling him to go the land of Zarephath where a widow woman would provide him with food and water.

Elijah made his way to Zarephath and when he got to the gates of the city, there was a widow woman just like God had said.

The woman was gathering sticks and he called to her and asked her to get him some water and some bread. The woman told Elijah that she did not have any bread. She told him that she only had a small amount of flour, oil and the sticks that she was taking back home to make a final meal for her and her son before they would starve to death.

Elijah told the woman to fear not as God has told him she will have enough flour and oil to feed him, her and her son until the Lord commands for rain to start falling again.

The woman went home and prepared the bread for Elijah and it was as he said: even after making bread for him there was enough for her and her son, and so it continued day after day.

Until one day the woman's son became very sick, and died. The woman thought Elijah had brought this sickness upon her son for something she had done wrong, but Elijah assured her that this was not the case.

He took the woman's son upstairs and laid him upon his bed, and began to cry out to the Lord.

Elijah prayed to God asking him to bring the boy back to life. The Lord God heard Elijah's prayers and the boy's life was restored once more.

Elijah brought the boy down to his mother and she rejoiced and said she now knows that Elijah is truly a man of God.

This Story teaches us that if we walk in fellowship with God and continue to obey him, He will always give us what we need and more, as His grace and mercy for us never runs out.

Elijah and the Prophets of Baal

(1 Kings 18-46)

In the third year of the drought, God again told Elijah to visit King Ahab.

When the King saw Elijah he blamed him for causing all the problems in Israel, but Elijah reminded him that it was him who had disobeyed all God's commandments and forsaken him for the false God Baal.

Elijah told King Ahab to bring all the Israelites and the prophets of Baal to Mount Carmel and when they arrived he told them that it was time for them to make up their minds once and for all as they could no longer worship God and Baal. He told them it was time for them to see which God was the true God, and if it was Baal then the people should worship him and if it was God then He should be worshipped.

Elijah told the prophets of Baal that they would both offer a sacrifice of a bull to their God's and whoever's God answered first with a sign of fire is surely the one true God.

So, the prophets of Baal set up their bull offering, and then called on the name of Baal hour after hour asking him to hear their cries, but still nothing happened.

Elijah prepared his offering by building an altar with twelve stones according to the tribes of the sons of Jacob. He covered the altar with wood, placed the bull on top and dug trenches around the altar. He poured water over the offering, which over flowed into the trenches.

Elijah called out the God of Israel, praying for Him to show the people that He was the one true God.

Then the fire of the Lord God came down and burnt the offering and licked up the water that was in the trench.

All the people that had gathered saw this and fell down on their faces and said the Lord, He is God.

Elijah told them to seize and kill all the prophets of Baal, making sure none of them escape.

Elijah then went up to the top of Mount Carmel and prayed for rain. Soon after the skies were black with clouds, wind and a great rain began to fall.

This story reminds us that there is only one God and that we should continue to worship our Lord God and not worship false idols in place of God. It is through our love for God that we will find victory and rewards.

The Story of Elisha

(1 Kings 2: 1-15)

As a young man, Elisha held Elijah in great regard and looked to him as his mentor and master.

Shortly before the Lord was about to take Elijah up to heaven in a whirlwind, Elijah was with Elisha and they were both on their way from the land of Gilgal.

Elijah knew that his time was near for the Lord to take him so he told Elisha to stay and not follow him to Bethel, but Elisha refused telling Elijah that he will not leave him.
Once again, on their way to Jericho, Elijah again asked Elisha not to accompany him, but again, Elisha refused.

As the two were about to cross the river Jordan, Elijah took his rolled up cloak and struck the water so that it divided to the right and the left allowing them to cross over dry land.

Finally, Elijah asked Elisha what he could do for him before he is taken, and Elisha asks for a double portion of Elijah's spirit. Elijah agrees to grant this to Elisha if Elisha can see him when he is taken by the Lord.

Suddenly, a chariot of fire and horses appeared, separating the two of them and taking Elijah up to heaven in a whirlwind.

Elisha saw what happened and cried out to the Lord as Elijah disappeared from his sight. Elisha then picked up Elijah's cloak that had fallen from him and struck the water with it asking where the Lord was.

The waters again divided to the right and the left, showing the prophets that Elisha had indeed been granted the double portion of Elisha's spirit that he had asked for.

When the prophets from Jericho saw what had happened, they acknowledged that the spirit of Elijah was resting on Elisha and they came and bowed before him.

This story shows how God knew how devoted Elijah was to serving others so he brought Elisha to him to train and take over his good work. We must always try to remember that God wants us to continue to spread his love to those that we meet.

Elisha and the Shunammite

(1 Kings 4: 8 -36)

One day whilst in the land of Shunem, Elisha was invited to the home of a childless wealthy woman who begged him to stay and eat with her and her husband. From that day on, whenever Elisha was in that area he would stop at the couple's house and have something to eat.

Now this woman knew that Elisha was a true prophet who served God, so she said to her husband that they should make up a small guest room for Elisha at the top of their house. In this room they put a table, chair, bed and lamp so that each time that Elisha visited he would have somewhere comfortable to stay.

During one of his visits, Elisha called his servant Gehazi and asked him to find out what he could do for this woman to repay her hospitality. When Gehazi told Elisha that the couple were childless and the woman's husband was old, he asked for the woman to be brought to him. Elisha told the Shunammite woman that this time the next year she would have a son. And just as Elisha had foretold, the woman gave birth to her son the following year.

A few years later, the child became ill and died on his mother's lap. The Shunammite immediately went up to the room where Elisha usually stayed and laid him on Elisha's bed. She then asked her husband to send a servant to accompany her to go to Elisha.

When Elisha returned to the Shunammite's home, he went to the room where the boy lay on the bed and closed the door behind him and his servant and the two of them prayed to the Lord. Elisha then lay down and stretched himself facing next to the boy, mouth to mouth, eyes to eyes and hands to hands and the boy grew warm, sneezing seven times and opened his eyes.

Elisha ordered Gehazi to call the Shunammite and when she came and saw her son alive, she fell at Elisha's feet and bowed to the ground.

Elisha Heals Namaan of Leprosy

(1 Kings 5: 1-14)

Within the land of Aram there was a great commander of the army, a man called Namaan who was highly regarded because through him, the Lord had given many victories. Although Namaan was a great warrior and soldier, he had leprosy and could not find a cure for this.

One day, a young Israelite girl, who had been taken captive and was now serving Namaan's wife, told her mistress that she knew of a prophet in Samaria who could cure Namaan of leprosy.

As soon as Namaan heard this, he told his master, the King of Aram, what the girl had said. The king willingly gave Namaan leave to go to Israel, telling him that he would also send him with a letter asking the King of Israel to cure Namaan of leprosy.

When Namaan presented himself to the King of Israel, he immediately thought that the King of Aram was testing him and trying to pick a quarrel. However, Elisha who had heard about Namaan's visit, sent a message to the king to send Namaan to him so that he will know that there is a prophet in Israel.

So Namaan took his horses and chariots and went to Elisha's house. On his arrival, Elisha sent a messenger out to him and told him that to cure his leprosy, he must wash himself in the river Jordan seven times. On hearing this, Namaan was angry, as he had expected Elisha to come and greet him personally and to pray to God to cure his leprosy. However, Namaan's servants urged him to do as he was instructed to, reminding him that if he had been asked to do a great deed to cure the leprosy he would have done it.

Namaan then went down and dipped himself in the river Jordan seven times and his flesh was restored and became clean again as if he had the flesh of a young boy.

Namaan and his servants went back to Elisha praising God and declaring that they now knew that there was no other God in the world than the God of Israel.

The Story of Elisha teaches us about humility and shows how through Elisha's acts of helpfulness this reminds us of God's love for His people. Our God wants us to always be willing to help others in their time of need and God will continue to bless us.

The Story of Daniel

(Daniel 1: 1-21)

After the king of Babylon had captured Jerusalem, the Lord also delivered the land of Judah into his hands. However, as he did not want to lose all of the noble and wise men from Judah, the King of Babylon ordered his official to choose some of the Israelites from the royal family -those of whom did not have any defects- were physically handsome, intelligent and also sufficiently qualified, to serve in the king's palace. The king then instructed that those Israelites selected should be trained for three years before being allowed to enter the king's palace. He also assigned them to be fed with a portion of food and wine from the king's table.

Amongst those chosen were four men including a man called Daniel. However because Daniel was raised to follow God's rule of not eating certain unholy meat, food and drink, Daniel felt that his body would be defiled if he ate the King of Babylon's royal food. Daniel therefore asked the chief official for permission not to eat the food.

Although God showed favour to Daniel and allowed the official to consider Daniel's request, the official still feared that the king would find out that he had not fed the men the food that had been allocated because the men would appear less healthy and weaker than the other men of his age.

Daniel then suggested that the official put his request to a test. So for ten days, Daniel and his comrades from Judah would be allowed to eat fruit and vegetables only, whilst the other young men would be given the royal food to eat.

At the end of the ten days, the official observed that Daniel and his comrades looked healthier and more nourished than any of the other men, so they were then allowed to continue eating the vegetables that they had chosen to eat.

God also gave these four men who were Daniel, Hanaiah, Mishael and Azariah great knowledge and wisdom of literature. He also gave Daniel the ability to understand all kinds of visions and dreams.

This story helps us to think about why God had rules about eating food and drink that is clean, healthy and good for our bodies. We should always remember that what we physically put into our bodies is just as important to us when we are following God's commands.

Daniel and the King of Babylon's Dream

(Daniel 2-3)

After the King of Babylon had reigned for a year, he began to have many dreams that troubled his mind, so much so that he could not sleep. The king who was called Nebuchadnezzar then sent an order saying that unless his dreams could be interpreted by the magicians, astrologers or sorcerers, they would be put to death. However, he declared that if anyone is able to tell the king his dream and what it means, he would give those men: gifts, rewards and great honour.

As none of the magicians, sorcerers and astrologers were able to help the king by interpreting his dream, he ordered that they all be put to death together with all the wise men in Babylon. When Daniel heard that the king had ordered his death, he asked to see the king to be given an opportunity to interpret the dream.

Daniel told Nebuchadnezzar that although the only one who can interpret his dream is by God in heaven, God has revealed the mysteries of the dreams to Daniel. Daniel described to the king a gigantic, dazzling, golden statue, which represented the king's dominion and power over his subjects.

King Nebuchadnezzar was pleased with Daniel and not only lavished him with gifts, he also made him the ruler over all the wise men in Babylon.
The king then made an image just like the one that had been in his dreams. This was an enormous statue made entirely of gold, which was over ninety feet tall and nine feet wide.
The king then gave an order to all his officials, governors, treasurers, magistrates and judges that whenever they hear the sound of the horn, flute, lyre, pipes or harp they must all fall down and worship the golden image. The king further instructed that if anyone disobeyed him they will be thrown into a blazing furnace.

One day Nebuchadnezzar was told that Hanaiah, Mishael and Azariah were not obeying his command for worshipping the statue so he ordered that they be thrown into the burning furnace. Hanaiah, Mishael and Azariah told the king that they were not afraid to be thrown into the furnace, as they are sure that they will be saved by their God in heaven who is the only God that they worship.

King Nebuchadnezzar then instructed that the furnace be heated seven times hotter than usual, however, just as Hanaiah, Mishael and Azariah had stated, they walked from the furnace alive. The king and his officials were amazed and the king praised the God of Israel decreeing that if anyone spoke against the God of Hanaiah, Mishael and Azariah that they would be cut to pieces.

This story shows how God humbled the King of Babylon by showing him that He is a faithful God who looks after those that serve Him. The story also shows that we must continue to worship God as no matter what, he will rescue us as our God is in control of everything so we should not lose our faith in God and follow what others want us to do.

Daniel in the Lion's Den

(Daniel 6: 1-26)

After king Nebuchadnezzar was driven from his kingdom and stripped of his glory, due to his arrogance and refusal to obey the Lord's commands, his son Belshazzar took his place on the throne. However, Belshazzar also did not honour God and so he was also not favoured by the Lord and eventually he was slain by Darius, who took over the kingdom.

As with Darius' predecessors, Daniel was highly regarded and given a high authority over his administration. This however made his fellow royal administrators jealous, as Daniel could do no wrong, so they set up a plan to turn the king against Daniel. They encouraged the king to set an official thirty-day rule whereby if anyone prayed to any God or man other than the king himself, then he will be thrown into the lion's den.

Although Daniel was aware of the ruling, he continued to pray to God asking for guidance. Hence the royal administrators went and told the king that Daniel had disregarded his ruling and was continuing to pray to God. This distressed Darius because he did not want any harm to come to Daniel, but the men urged him to make an example of Daniel.

The king therefore ordered that Daniel be thrown into the lion's den, saying to Daniel, "may your God who you serve continually, rescue you."

The king then placed a stone over the mouth of the lion's den and returned troubled to his palace.

The following morning when the king went to the lion's den and called out for Daniel, Daniel answered him and told him that he had not been harmed by the lions. Daniel also said that God had shut the mouths of the lions because he was innocent and had not done anything wrong to the king.

The king was so overjoyed that he gave orders for Daniel to be brought out of the den and instead threw the men who had falsely accused Daniel in the den along with their families, all of whom were immediately overpowered and killed by the lions.

'Darius also issued a decree that everyone in his kingdom must fear and worship the God that Daniel worships'.

This story reminds us that we must remain faithful to God at all times and even when others try to find ways to dampen our faith, we must remain true because when we are in our darkest hour of need, God will remain faithful to us and rescue us.

The Story of Jonah

(Jonah 1-4)

There was once a Hebrew man called Jonah who was the son of Amittai. One day the Lord came to Jonah and told him to go and preach to the city of Nineveh.This was because God had had enough of how wicked the people who lived there behaved. However Jonah was afraid to go and did not do as the Lord had asked and instead he tried to run away by boarding a ship heading for the port of Toppa.

The Lord was angry at what Jonah had done so he sent a violent storm with such heavy winds that the ship was at risk of breaking up. All of the sailors on the ship were so afraid that they each cried out to their own gods to save them and they even threw some of the cargo off the ship to lighten its load.

Jonah, however had gone below deck and in his fear had fallen into a deep sleep. The sailors were amazed that he could sleep at this time, so they woke him up and asked him to pray to his God to calm the seas so that they would not perish.

The sailors also wanted to know who was responsible for what had happened to them, so they tried to find out more about Jonah asking him who he was and where he had come from. They also asked Jonah to tell them who he thought was responsible for bringing such a heavy storm to to them and why this had happened?

Jonah told them that he was a Hebrew, who worshipped the God of heaven and earth and that it was his God who made the sea and the land. Jonah also told them why he had decided to run away and said that this was why the Lord was angry and had caused the great storm to come because Jonah had not done as the Lord had asked.

Jonah then told the sailors that as it was his fault they should throw him into the sea and it will become calm.

Although the men were afraid, they did not want to be responsible for Jonah's death. But eventually they had no choice and so they threw Jonah overboard, asking God not to hold them accountable if he was innocent. Immediately the raging sea calmed and the sailors were in awe of the Lord, making vows and offering Him a sacrifice.

When Jonah was thrown overboard instead of allowing him to simply drown, the Lord sent a great big whale to swallow him up whole.

Jonah remained in the belly of the whale for three days and three nights and during this time he prayed deeply to God, thanking him for not allowing him to die. Jonah was very grateful for his life and acknowledged that despite his disobedience, the Lord was still willing to save him. So he asked the Lord to forgive him for not listening to Him and for not doing what the Lord had asked of him. Jonah made a vow to God and promised that he would serve the Lord as salvation comes only from the Lord.

On hearing Jonah's prayer, the Lord commanded the whale to set Jonah free and the whale immediately spat out Jonah onto dry land.

This time when God spoke to Jonah asking him to return to the city of Nineveh to share the Lord's message about how unhappy God was because of their wicked ways, Jonah obeyed the Lord and set off for the city of Nineveh.

When Jonah arrived at Nineveh, he spoke to the people telling them that after forty days the Lord would overturn their city because of their wicked ways. However because the Ninevite people believed in God they immediately repented, put on sackcloth and declared a fast, pleading for God's forgiveness.

To demonstrate their commitment to God the king of Nineveh also issued a declaration decreeing that neither man or beast should break the fast and in this way, God might decide to show them compassion and not allow them to die.

When God saw how the inhabitants of Nineveh had turned from their evil ways He had compassion and decided to let them live and not to bring about their destruction. Jonah was very unhappy about this as he felt that the people should be punished. Jonah then went off and waited for the destruction of Nineveh. He sat in the shade where God had also provided a vine to ease his discomfort in the sun.Jonah reminded God that he had not wanted to tell the Ninevites what God had told him to tell them which is why he had run away and felt that now God should follow through on what he had said that he would do.

God therefore questioned Jonah about his right to be angry and reminded him that he had shown compassion to Jonah when he had requested it, yet Jonah now expected him not to show the same compassion to a city of more than a hundred and twenty thousand people.

This story reminds us that our God is a forgiving God and that even after we have done bad things and disobeyed God, if we ask God for forgiveness and show Him that we have repented, then He will show us compassion.

NEW TESTAMENT

A girl named Mary

(Luke 1:26-38)

Many years ago, God sent the Angel Gabriel to Nazareth, a city of Galilee, where a young girl called Mary lived. At this time Mary was engaged to be married to a man called Joseph who worked as a carpenter.

The Angel Gabriel told Mary that she was highly favoured, because the Lord was with her. He also said that she was blessed among women because the Lord had chosen her.

Now, when Mary saw the angel she was scared by what he had told her, for she did not understand what type of greeting this was. However, Angel Gabriel knew that she was frightened and told her not to fear, because she had found favour with God. He told Mary that she would conceive and have a child, who she should call Jesus. Gabriel also told Mary that her son Jesus would be great and that he would be called the Son of God. He said that the Lord God would give Jesus the throne of his father David, and that He would reign over the house of Jacob, and there would be no end to His kingdom.

Mary questioned Angel Gabriel about how she could be with child, as she was a virgin. But the Angel Gabriel told her that the child conceived in her would be of the Holy Spirit. He will overshadow her, and the child will also be called the Son of God. Mary was really happy that God had chosen her. She rejoiced and declared herself a servant of the Lord, and accepted all that God had asked of her. Mary praised the Lord, thanking him that He had blessed her even though she had come from a poor family, to carry His son Jesus whilst acknowledging that God is a mighty, and loving God.

The Angel Gabriel told Mary that God had also blessed her cousin Elizabeth who was barren and was now quite old. However, as nothing is impossible for God, Elizabeth would also give birth to a son as she was six months pregnant.

This story shows us that we don't have to be rich and come from a high status for God to decide that He wants to use us in His plans. God chose Mary to play one of the most important roles ever, which was to carry His Son, Jesus Christ. Mary humbly accepted what God had asked her to do, although she was still a virgin and was engaged to be married to Joseph who also willingly accepted that God had asked his wife to carry His son.

Mary and Elizabeth

(Luke 1:39-44)

Six months before the Angel Gabriel had come to Mary, he had spoken to the priest Zacharias, the husband of Elizabeth who is Mary's first cousin. Both Zacharias and Elizabeth were very old, and Elizabeth was barren, so they did not have any children. The Angel Gabriel had come to tell Zacharias that his prayer concerning having children was answered, for Elizabeth would have a son, and they should call him John.

However, because Zacharias had doubted what he had been told, the Angel Gabriel stopped Zacharias from being able to speak due to his disbelief, telling him that he would remain dumb until all he had declared had happened.

Soon after the Angel Gabriel had spoken to Mary, she hurried into the city of Judah to the home of Zacharias and Elizabeth. Mary greeted Elizabeth, and just as the angel Gabriel had said, when Elizabeth heard Mary, her baby leapt in the womb because she was filled with the Holy Spirit. Elizabeth knew that Mary was carrying the Lord Jesus, for her baby leapt in her womb at the sound of her voice.

Before she left to return home, both Elizabeth and Mary praised and magnified God and the Lord Jesus.

Again just as the Angel Gabriel had stated, 3 months later Elizabeth gave birth to a son. All her neighbours and relatives were so happy that they rejoiced that the Lord had shown such mercy by granting her a son.

As was the Jewish practice when it came to name the child, everyone thought that Elizabeth and Zacharias would name their son Zacharias after his father. However, because he could not speak, Zacharias wrote the name 'John' on a writing tablet for all that God had done.

This story reminds us that when God asks us to do something we must be joyful that He has chosen us and not fearful. We must trust in God when He tells us something, as disbelief which Zacharias had, can ruin our blessing. God is able to do all things. When He says something, He does not lie, no matter how impossible it may sound or look.

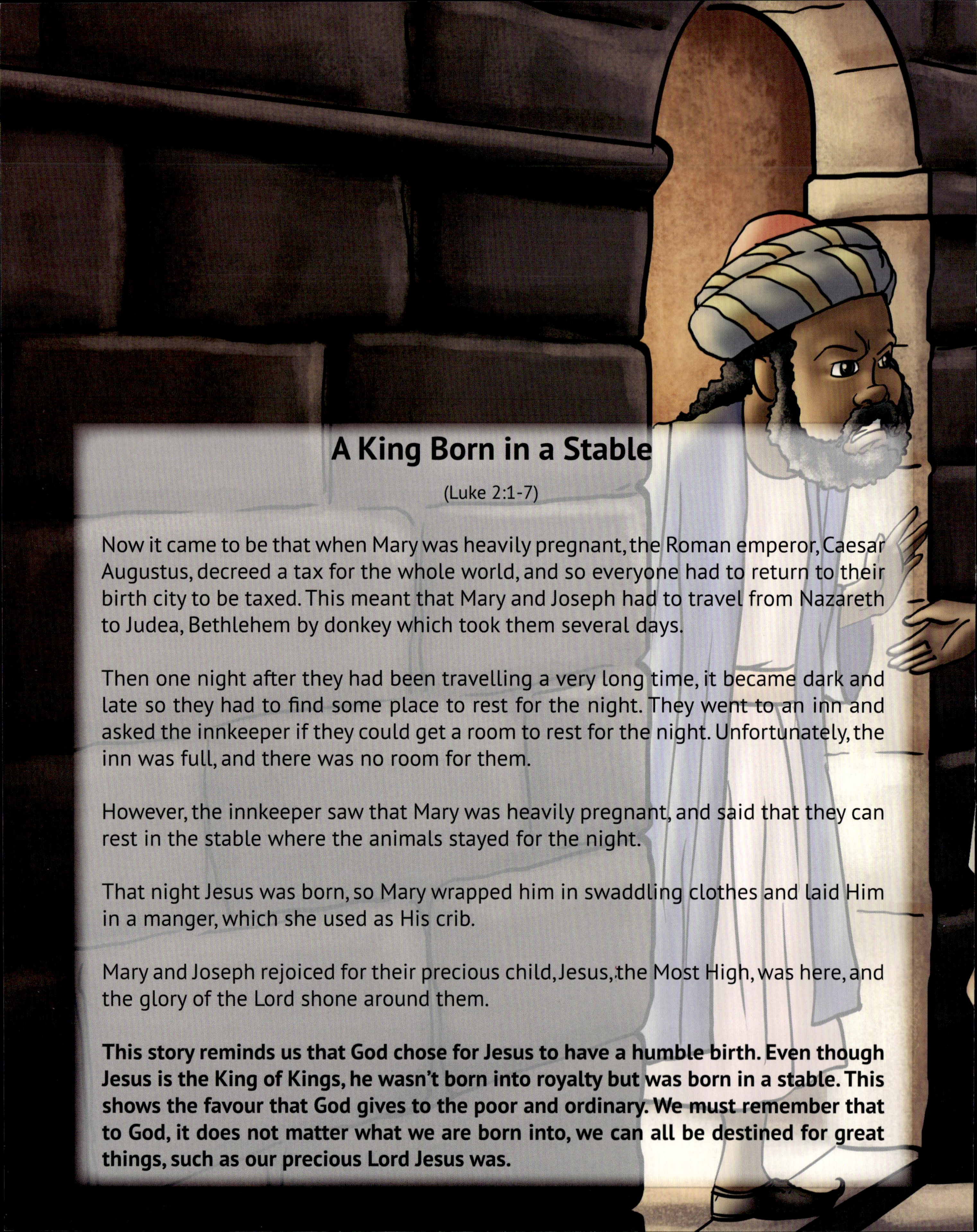

A King Born in a Stable

(Luke 2:1-7)

Now it came to be that when Mary was heavily pregnant, the Roman emperor, Caesar Augustus, decreed a tax for the whole world, and so everyone had to return to their birth city to be taxed. This meant that Mary and Joseph had to travel from Nazareth to Judea, Bethlehem by donkey which took them several days.

Then one night after they had been travelling a very long time, it became dark and late so they had to find some place to rest for the night. They went to an inn and asked the innkeeper if they could get a room to rest for the night. Unfortunately, the inn was full, and there was no room for them.

However, the innkeeper saw that Mary was heavily pregnant, and said that they can rest in the stable where the animals stayed for the night.

That night Jesus was born, so Mary wrapped him in swaddling clothes and laid Him in a manger, which she used as His crib.

Mary and Joseph rejoiced for their precious child, Jesus, the Most High, was here, and the glory of the Lord shone around them.

This story reminds us that God chose for Jesus to have a humble birth. Even though Jesus is the King of Kings, he wasn't born into royalty but was born in a stable. This shows the favour that God gives to the poor and ordinary. We must remember that to God, it does not matter what we are born into, we can all be destined for great things, such as our precious Lord Jesus was.

The Strangers Follow a Star

(Luke 2:8-20)

After the birth of Jesus, some shepherds were tending to their sheep in a field nearby when an angel of the Lord came to them and they were afraid.
The angel told them not to be afraid telling them, "behold! I bring you good news of great joy, which shall be good news to all people." The angel then told them that Mary had given birth to a Saviour, who is Christ the Lord and that the child would be found lying in a manger wrapped in swaddling clothes.

Suddenly a whole multitude of angels appeared also praising God, saying, "glory to God in the highest and on earth, peace and goodwill towards men."
The shepherds were in awe and once the angels had left they decided to go and seek out what they had been told by the angels of the Lord.

By following the bright star that shone brightly around the stable where Jesus was born, the shepherds soon found Mary, Joseph and, just as the angel had told them, Jesus lying in a manger in swaddling clothes.

The shepherds were amazed at what they had seen and returned home praising God and glorifying His name to everyone that they saw, both near and far.

Now there were some wise men who were travelling from the East to Jerusalem as they had heard about the birth of Jesus Christ. They had seen the star in the East and had sent word asking where the child that was born the 'King of the Jews' was, as they wanted to come to worship Jesus. Stars normally go from East to West but this, being a star of the Lord, followed to the East.

The wise men also followed the star, which went before them to the East until it led them to where the young child, Jesus, was. They had travelled day and night, following the star, for it stayed bright before them, every step of the way.

When the star stood over the stable where Jesus lay in a manger, the wise men rejoiced with exceeding joy, for they knew that the Lord was here.

The wise men went into the stable, fell down and worshipped Jesus. They had brought with them treasure for the young child and they laid before Jesus: gifts of gold, frankincense and myrrh.

This story reminds us that Jesus Christ is most worthy to be praised. Even when Jesus was a baby, only days old, and was lying in a manager in a stable, wise men fell down and worshipped at His feet. At all times we must worship Jesus as the precious Son of God, because no matter who we are and where we are, He deserves it. The wise men, who were rich kings, travelled all the way from the east to Jerusalem, just to see Jesus. This was worth all their time and effort, as it should be for us. We should do everything we can to spend time with our Lord, Jesus Christ.

Herod the King

(Matthew 2:1-17)

Now before the wise men had followed the star to Jerusalem, King Herod had also heard about the birth of Jesus Christ and he was very troubled because he heard that Jesus would be the King of all kings. Herod called all the chief priests and scribes demanding that they tell him where the Christ had been born.

The chief priests and scribes told Herod that it had been written by the prophets that the ruler of all Israel would be born in Bethlehem, which was in the land of Judah.

Herod had therefore spoken to the wise men privately to enquire about the star, which shone so bright for the Christ child, asking them what time it had appeared. Afterwards, King Herod had sent the wise men to Bethlehem telling them that as soon as they found the young child they should bring word to him so that he could also come and worship Jesus.

Herod however, had no to desire to worship the baby Jesus, but to destroy Him. He thought that Jesus would take over all he had and wanted.

The wise men were warned by God in a dream that they should not return to King Herod to let him know where Jesus lay, so they had departed back to their own city using another route.

After the wise men had gone, an angel of the Lord had appeared to Joseph in a dream. The angel told him that he should take Mary and his son and flee to Egypt as Herod was seeking to destroy Jesus.

Joseph waited until night fell and he gathered his young child and Mary and without anyone's knowledge, they all departed for Egypt.

Once King Herod realised that the wise men had deceived him, he was extremely angry. He came up with an evil plan, and ordered that all the baby boys under the age of two, who were in living in Bethlehem, be killed. Not realising that God knows all things, and knew of King Herod's plan before he even thought it. Hence Joseph and Mary had already left Bethlehem after God had sent one of his angels to Joseph telling him to flee with his family into Egypt until the angel brought word that they would be safe from King Herod.

There was great weeping, sorrow and mourning for the death of all the young children who Herod had slain, but because Joseph trusted in the Lord and followed His warning, and straight away fled into Egypt, Jesus was safe.

This story reminds us that there can be evil people such as Herod the King, who have evil plans, such as killing all the baby boys. However, God knows all things, and because He loves and cares for us, God will warn and protect us from all evil. But we must make sure that we listen to God, and follow His instructions straightaway. Even if we do not understand, God is only trying to protect us from what we do not see yet; if we delay in following God's instructions, we may be putting ourselves into danger.

The Boy in the Temple

(Luke 2:1-17)

Every year Jesus, Mary and Joseph went from their home in Nazareth to Jerusalem to attend the feast of the Passover.

On this particular year, when Jesus was 12 years of age, as usual, they went to Jerusalem after the custom of the feast.

The family spent their time there until it was time to go back home with all of the friends and relatives who were also returning home. However, unbeknown to his parents, Jesus had stayed behind in Jerusalem, whilst His parents had set off on their way home. In fact, the crowd of people that returned home to Nazareth from Jerusalem was so huge, that Mary and Joseph did not yet know that Jesus was not with them.

So thinking that Jesus was amongst the crowd, His parents, continued on their way for a day. They then tried to find Jesus among their family and friends, but they couldn't see Him, so they had to return to Jerusalem.

Having journeyed back to Jerusalem, and looking for Jesus, for three days, they eventually came to find Jesus in the temple.Jesus was sitting in the middle of a group of doctors, listening intently to them and also asking them questions. Everyone in the temple that heard what Jesus was speaking about were amazed and shocked at Jesus' understanding and answers.

When Mary and Joseph saw Jesus there they were also amazed, and Jesus' mother said to Him, "why have you done this to us, see how your father and I have been looking for you in sorrow?" For Mary and Joseph did not know what had happened to Jesus and were frantic with worry.

Jesus replied to his mother, "why were you looking for me, didn't you know that I must be in my Father's house?"

For Jesus from the age of 12 had started to do what He was brought into the earth to do: God's will. However, Mary and Joseph did not understand what he was saying. Jesus then listened and obeyed His mother by returning back to Nazareth, and He was subject to His parents. But his mother, Mary, kept what he had said in her heart. As Jesus grew in both his size and wisdom, He remained in great favour with both God and man.

This story reminds us that Jesus was put onto this earth for our heavenly Father's will, and not to do his own things. Although no one else understood, not even Jesus' natural parents, Jesus knew for himself. It also reminds us that Jesus was faithful and obedient to His parents because he was still a child. He could have stayed at the temple longer, but chose to obey his natural parents, as he chooses to obey our Father in heaven. This is a lesson to ourselves, to follow Jesus' example and follow our parents until we are old enough to hear God's instructions to us. As children we have to be very obedient when we are young and not go against our parents instructions.

Jesus' Baptism

(Matthew 3:13-17)

As was foretold, John the son of Zacharias and Elizabeth, had grown up to be a very faithful servant to the Lord and had become known as John the Baptist, as he preached God's glory far and wide into the wilderness of Judah, preparing the way for Jesus. John was known by his clothing of camel hair and the leather belt that he always wore, and many came to him confessing their sins and were baptised in the river of Jordan.

One day Jesus came down from Nazareth of Galilee to the river Jordan to be baptised by John. When Jesus arrived, John was able to realise that this stranger was Jesus, the Son of God, because it had been written and John was filled with the Holy Ghost. John was confused as to why Jesus came to him to be baptised, when in fact Jesus is the Saviour of all who should instead be baptising him.

Jesus explained to John, that he must grant him His desire because God sent John ahead of him to baptise Jesus, and so God's word should be fulfilled. For this reason John baptised Jesus.

After Jesus was baptised He straightaway came out of the water and the heavens were opened to Him. Jesus saw the Spirit of God coming down like a dove, and lightening on Him.

A voice from heaven said, "this is my beloved Son, in whom I am well pleased."

This story reminds us that even Jesus was baptised, and our Father in heaven was pleased. Likewise, we should also be baptised when we can, in obedience to God's instruction, and Jesus' example. Jesus' baptism was full immersion in the river Jordan and it was his desire. This is our example of how we should be baptised: fully immersed and by our own choice and desire, knowing what it means to be baptised. John also didn't understand why Jesus asked him to baptise Him, the Son of God. But God may not always ask us to do things that we understand, but just as John was obedient to Jesus, we should be too.

The Temptation of Jesus

(Matthew 4:1-11)

Immediately after being baptised, being full of the Holy Spirit, Jesus returned from Jordan and was led by the Holy Spirit into the wilderness where He remained in the wilderness for 40 days, to be tempted by the devil. During those days Jesus did not eat anything, he fasted 40 days and 40 nights and thereafter he was very hungry.

The devil knew that because of his hunger Jesus would be vulnerable, so he came to Jesus in an effort to tempt Him and said, 'if you are the Son of God, command that these stones be made into bread'.

Jesus stood firm and answered, "it is written, that man shall not live by bread alone, but by every word that comes out of the mouth of God."

The devil then took Jesus on the pinnacle of the temple above a holy city and said, "if you are the Son of God cast yourself down: for it is written, He shall give his angels charge concerning thee: and in their hands, they shall hold you up, in case at any time you strike your foot against a stone."

Jesus said to him, "it is written again, you shalt not tempt the Lord your God and put him to a test."

Again, the devil took Jesus to an exceedingly high mountain and showed Him all the kingdoms of the world and their glory. The devil said to Jesus, "all these things I will give you, if you will bow down and worship me."

Jesus did not waiver, instead he said to the devil, "get thee behind me, Satan: for it is written, Worship the Lord your God, and serve Him only."

And when the devil had ended all the temptation, he departed from Jesus and the angels came and attended to Jesus.

This story reminds us that sometimes the Holy Spirit may put us into situations to test us, so we are able to grow and develop. It was only after passing this test of temptation, of 40 days by the devil, that Jesus started performing miracles. A test of temptation may be our only obstacle to progressing to another stage closer to what God created us to be. Jesus overcame the devil with the word of God, which is our example. We must always use God's word, which never lies, to be our weapon. But we can only use God's word if we know it, and so we need to spend our time reading God's words, and learning His promises. Also, when we have passed our test of temptation, God will send his angels to speak goodness to us, as He did Jesus.

Jesus Performs Water in to Wine Miracle

(John 2:1-11)

One day, there was a wedding that took place in Cana of Galilee. Mary, the mother of Jesus, was invited with Jesus and His disciples, who were also called to attend the ceremony.

The guests were celebrating but wanted more wine, as there was none left. Jesus' mother Mary spoke to Him telling Him that they have no more wine. However, Jesus told her that this is it not to do with him yet, as it is not his time to intervene.

Mary then replies in belief and reverence for her child, knowing Him to be the Son of God, and saying to the servants, "whatsoever he tells you, you do it."

Nearby there were six large stone water pots set before Jesus. Each large enough to hold several gallons of water which the Jews used for ceremonial washing.

Jesus told the servants to fill the water pots up with water and the servants filled them up to the brim. Jesus then told them to take the water pots and serve it out to the master of the ceremonial feast. And in obedience the servants served the water as instructed.

When the master of the feast tasted the water that was made wine and did not know where it had come from, as only the servants knew, he called the bridegroom to him. The master of the feast said, "most people usually serve the good wine first, leaving the poor wine until after everyone has had enough, yet you have saved the best wine 'til the end." For Jesus had turned the water to wine.

This story reminds us that there is a time for Jesus to intervene in everything, and that we cannot rush God. It is our duty to remain in belief that something we have asked for will be done by God, even if it is not straightaway, when we ask. This is the start of Jesus' miracles, all of which manifested the glory of our Father in heaven.

The Twelve Disciples

(Matthew 4:18-22)

Jesus chose his closest followers very carefully because He wanted men that He could trust to deliver God's messages, even when He would no longer be around to lead them. Jesus chose twelve disciples in total to follow and learn from Him.

Simon Peter, known as Peter, and his brother Andrew were the first disciples that Jesus chose. One day when He was walking by the sea of the Galilee, He saw the two fishermen, Peter, and his brother Andrew, casting a net into the sea.

Jesus entered Peter's ship, sat down and began to teach and speak. Then Jesus told Peter to cast out their net into the sea, even though they had worked and not caught anything all night, and Peter obeyed, believing in Jesus. When he cast down the net they caught a multitude of fishes, and their net was so filled that it broke.

Jesus said to them, "follow me, and I will make you fishers of men."

Peter and Andrew straightaway left their nets and followed Jesus. Jesus then walked on and saw two other men, James the son of Zebedee and John his brother. James and John were in the ship with Zebedee, their father, mending their nets. Jesus called them and they immediately left the ship, and their father, and followed Him.

The next day, Jesus went into Galilee, and found Philip. Jesus told Philip to follow Him. Then Jesus found Thomas, who is sometimes called 'doubting Thomas'.

Jesus then went from his own city, and saw a man named Matthew, the publican, sitting at the receipt of custom. Jesus told Matthew, "follow me", and Matthew straightaway rose and followed Him.

The names of the other disciples of Jesus are: Bartholomew, Thomas, James, the son of Alphaeus, Thaddaeus, Simon the Canaanite and finally Judah Iscariot who was the one who came to betray Jesus leading up to His death.

This story reminds us that Jesus chose us and that we did not choose Him. When he tells us to follow Him to be close to God, we must follow Him. When Jesus tells us to do something He may only tell us once, so we need to arise straightaway and follow Him.

The Lessons that Jesus teaches Outside

(Matthew 5:1-48)

One day Jesus leaves the multitudes of people that He was preaching to and goes up to the mountains. His disciples follow Him and Jesus teaches them a lot of important lessons.

Jesus reminds them about following the Laws of Moses that says, 'you must not kill'. Jesus tells them that the same judgement that someone receives for murder is the same judgement someone will receive for being angry with someone without a just reason. Jesus explains that the only just reason to show anger is if it is against God. He told the disciples that they must all be slow to become angry, as when anyone is angry with someone they must reconcile their differences before they can go to God freely.

Jesus also talks about temptation, and says, "you must not commit adultery".

However, He also said that a person looking at someone with lust is committing adultery in their heart, and so the same judgement will apply as if they had actually committed adultery. Jesus said that is better to cut off any part of the body that may cause you to fall into temptation, than to keep it and lose your whole body to hell.

Jesus then talks about divorce, saying that a husband should not divorce his wife as God values marriage. When two come together they are made as one in the eyes of the Lord and he does not want any man to separate what He has put together, unless they have been unfaithful.

Jesus reminds His disciples that they must not make any oaths as the words you speak should be valued as honest, and so they should not swear on anything. He tells them not to swear on heaven for it is God's throne, and not to swear on earth, for it is God's footstall. He also says that you should not swear on yourself, because you are not in control. But let all things you say be as you do, as anything more than this is evil.

Jesus then talks to the disciples about forgiveness saying that we must not seek revenge, as revenge belongs to God only. He says that we must love and forgive, and so when someone does wrong against us, we should love them. And we must give to those who ask, and lend to those who want to borrow.

According to Jesus we must love our enemies, bless them, pray for them and do good to them. He says that our response to their actions may show our hearts of love, and that God who is love, lives in us. Jesus tells us that we cannot just love those who love us, because we are different and set apart by God, so we should love all, even if they do not love us.

Jesus teaches the disciples about giving, saying that when they give, it must not be in vain to show off their righteousness. He says that when they give they must not seek a reward, or do it for their own gain, but to give from within because of the love in their hearts.

Jesus also says that we must forgive others to be forgiven, as this stops the burden to go before God freely.

This story reminds us that Jesus is such an example for us all. Jesus always wants to teach us what we need to do so that we can become good and faithful servants of God. Jesus never taught anything that He did not live, and Jesus on earth lived to follow the will of our Father in heaven. We must follow Jesus as our example and live to be like Him.

Jesus teaches 'The Lord's Prayer'

(Matthew 6:9-15)

Jesus spoke to his disciples about how important prayer is to God, and He taught them how they must pray. He said that they should not pray in vain, or in front of others to appear righteous and to be seen by men. He tells them that they must pray to seek God and to be close to Him in communication.

Jesus reminded the disciples that God, our Father, sees what is done in secret and will reward you accordingly. So when you pray, it should not be done like a babbling pagan, believing that the more words that are spoken will make God hear, as God knows what they need even before they ask.

Jesus provided the disciples with a prayer structure, which consists of thanksgiving and provision and this is Jesus' prayer:

Our Father in heaven, Hallowed be your name.
Your kingdom come, your will be done on earth, as it is in heaven.
Give us this day our daily bread.
And forgive us our debts, as we forgive our debtors.
And lead us not into temptation, but deliver us from evil:
For thine is the kingdom, and the power, and the glory, for ever, Amen.

The Lord's Prayer shows us that we have to acknowledge that God is our Father, He loves us, and we are His children. He is our Father, meaning we are all brothers and sisters in Christ, and so therefore we have to love others as we love ourselves. 'Hallowed be thy name' is admitting that our Father is holy. Only He is perfect, and we must always enter into prayer glorifying God and providing thanksgiving. We ask for God's kingdom to come on earth, that it may be more like heaven, and a better place to live. Pray for our daily bread. We have new challenges each day, and so God provides us with new strength to get through each day at a time. We must forgive others, the same way that our Father in heaven forgives us. We pray that God does not lead us into the path of temptation, but to deliver us from evil. To get us through the trials and temptations we must acknowledge that the kingdom of heaven is God's, and He is worthy of all the glory and power.

This story reminds us that Jesus is our perfect example, for He never sinned and He completely followed the will of our Father in heaven. Jesus gives us an example of how to pray, and so we use the example to structure our own prayers to be effective in our praying. Jesus always wants to help and guide us, so we need to make sure we follow the example.

The Wise and Foolish Builders

(Matthew 7: 24-29)

Whilst preaching His Sermon on the Mount, Jesus told the story about two builders to illustrate the lessons that Jesus was trying to teach. Jesus was showing that the outcome is depending on whether we hear and put into practice Jesus' word, or if we decide not to do what He teaches us.

Jesus said that if we listen and do God's teachings, we are wise and have built our house on a rock, which is a strong and solid foundation.

Hence the rain will fall, the flood will come and the wind will blow and beat on the house. But the house will not fall because the house was built on a strong, unmoving rock.

However, everyone who hears God's teachings but does not put it into practice is like the foolish man, who builds his house on sand.

Hence the rain will fall, the flood will come and the wind will blow and beat on the house and the house will simply fall, with a great crash.

After Jesus had spoken, the crowds were amazed at his teachings and the authority with which he spoke.

This story reminds us of how important it is to hear and do God's teachings. The rain, flood and wind represents the hard times that we face and the trial and temptation that we will all have to deal with. If we do as God tells us it means that we build our lives on Jesus, who is our rock that is always the same, and dependable. And so when we face hard times, we can rest upon the rock of Jesus, and use the lessons he has taught us. However, if we do not do as God tells us, we do not have any foundation, and so when hard times come we will fall, because we cannot lean upon Jesus, our rock.

The Story of the Paralysed Man (Palsy man)

(Matthew 9: 1-8)

One day Jesus was teaching and entered a ship that had come into His own city and into Capernaum. Immediately many were gathered to see and hear from Jesus, so that His whole surrounding was packed out.

Some men hearing that Jesus was there, brought a man paralysed with palsy lying on a bed. However, as they couldn't come near because of the crowd surrounding Jesus, they went onto the housetop, uncovered the roof of the place, and when they had broken it, they lowered down the bed through the tiling, in the midst of Jesus. Jesus seeing their faith said to the one sick of palsy, "be of good cheer, your sins are forgiven of you."

On hearing what Jesus said, certain scribes said to themselves, "this man is blaspheming!'

But Jesus could hear their thoughts and asked why they have evil in their hearts? Jesus then said, "is it easier to say your sins be forgiven or to say, get up and walk?"

However in order to let them know that the Son of Man has authority on earth to forgive sins, Jesus then told the paralysed man to arise, take his mat and go home. And the man rose up and went home.

When the crowd saw what Jesus had done, they were filled with amazement and they began to praise God, who had given his authority to Jesus.

This story reminds us that we need to be passionate for Jesus, and that even though there may be things that block us from Jesus, we must overcome using our passion to be in the presence of God. Faith is very important and our faith is shown in our actions. We learn from this story that everyone was probably wondering why Jesus said, 'your sins are forgiven', when they came for healing. The truth is that Jesus died for our sins and so He can forgive all our sins. Forgiving our sins in more important than healing, because it means a true relationship with God can occur. It also shows that Jesus has the authority to forgive sins, because He will be dying for them.

Jesus Calms the Storm

(Matthew 8:23-27)

As Jesus continued to preach the crowds continued to grow, so much so that Jesus gave orders to cross over to the other side of the lake, as by now Jesus was tired and was seeking somewhere to rest his head.

Jesus then went onto a ship and the disciples followed Him, and they went on their journey.

After they had been travelling a while, there started a great and furious storm where the waves beat onto the ship and covered the ship, so that it was now full of water. It was a scary storm, which made the disciples begin to start panicking. Jesus was however in the bottom part of the ship, fast asleep.

The disciples were so scared that they went and woke Jesus saying to Him, "Master, save us! Do you not care if we drown?"

Jesus rose and rebuked the wind, and said to the sea, "peace, be still." The wind and sea obeyed Jesus and became still, and there was a great calm.

Jesus then asked the disciples, "why are you so fearful? How do you not have any faith?"

The disciples, amazed at how powerful Jesus was, asked themselves, "what kind of a man is this that even the wind and sea obeyed His order?"

This story reminds us that God is with us no matter what. It also shows that even in really hard times, when it feels like we are going through a storm and it feels like God is sleeping on us, we need to believe in God's power and have faith. We also need to realise that God knows everything, and so if He knows that we are in danger, He will intervene. We need to trust in His awesome power, and know God will not put us through more than we can bear. God is always with us, even when it feels like He is absent, we do not need to fear, but we should continue to trust Him.

Jesus Talks with a Samaritan Woman

(John 4: 1-26)

When Jesus learned that the Pharisees were troubled because He was baptising more disciples than John the Baptist, He decided to return to Galilee.

Now on the journey from Judaea to Galilee, He had to go through Samaria and He came to the city of Samaria called Sychar. Soon, Jesus approached a plot of land that Jacob had given to his son Joseph, where Jacob's well was. Jesus had a long journey and so being fatigued, He sat at the well.

It was around the 6th hour of the day when a woman of Samaria came to draw water and Jesus asked her to get Him a drink, for He was without His disciples, who had gone to get food.

The woman of Samaria was very confused as Jesus, being a Jew, had asked for a drink from her. For at this time no Jew would speak, deal with or even be in the same presence as a Samaritan, because of their dislike for another.

Jesus answered, "if you knew what a gift of God it is that I am speaking to you, because of who I am, you would have asked for water from me, and I would have given you living water."

The woman did not understand and replied in confusion saying, "you do not have anything to draw water with so where are you going to get the living water from? Is your water better than the water of Jacob?"

And Jesus replied to her saying, "who drinks the water of Jacob will thirst again, but whoever drinks the living water will never thirst, but will lead to everlasting life." The woman, then in faith, asks Jesus to give her the living water so that she will never thirst.

Jesus then tells her to call her husband, knowing her sin. And she said she does not have a husband, which is the truth, but conceals the whole truth. Jesus is all knowing, and tells her that she has had 5 husbands and the man she is now with is not her husband. Jesus reveals her sin and so reveals that He has the power to know. The woman from Samaria then realised that Jesus is a prophet, for He was able to tell her what she had not told Him.

The woman says, "I know that the Messiah, called Christ, is coming, and when He does, He will tell us all things."

Jesus then replied, "I am Him, who is speaking to you."

By this time, Jesus' disciples had returned, but did not say anything about Jesus talking with the Samaritan woman.

The woman from Samaria, however left her water pot and returned to her city marvelling at what she had been told by Jesus and telling everyone to come and see the man who had told her things that she had not spoken about, stating, "is this not the Christ?"

This story reminds us that Jesus came to save us from our sins. It does not matter who we are and what we have done, but Jesus came for us so that we will be set free. We will be set free and forgiven when we repent of our sins, and accept Jesus as our Lord and Saviour. It is God's grace that saves us and not our own works, religion or traditions.

Lord of the Sabbath

(Matthew 12: 1-14)

It was a Sabbath day and Jesus and His disciples were walking through the cornfields. His disciples were hungry and so they began to pluck the ears of the corn and eat. The Pharisees saw this and accused the disciples of being unlawful because they saw this as the disciples working on the Sabbath day.

Jesus responded to the Pharisees using King David as an example, saying that when King David and his men were hungry, he entered into the house of God and ate the showbread, which was meant for only the priests to eat.

Jesus told the Pharisees that He is much more than King David, He is the Son of God. Then Jesus said, "the Sabbath was made for man, and not man for the Sabbath. Therefore, the Son of man is also the Lord even on the Sabbath."

Jesus then left and went into their synagogue. Whilst there, a man came to Jesus with a withered hand. And the Pharisees tried to trick and accuse Jesus by asking him if it was lawful to heal on the Sabbath.

Jesus responds asking them whether any of them would help to rescue their own sheep, which had fallen into a pit, rather than leave it there, even on the Sabbath. Jesus then said, "is a man worth more than a sheep?" And asked, "is it lawful to do good or evil on the Sabbath? To save lives, or to kill?"

Jesus then told the man to stretch his hand to Him and when the man stretched for His hand, Jesus restored it whole, like his other hand.

This story reminds us that Jesus is Lord over everything, even the Sabbath day. That Jesus has set us free from the law, the religious acts and rules, for salvation but all who believe in Him as Lord and Saviour may have everlasting life. We should always do as God says, which is to love others as yourself, even if it goes against rules and religious acts, because to love one another is what Jesus tells us, and shows us in His sacrifice for us.

Jesus is the Good Shepherd

(John 10: 1-21)

Disillusioned by what the Pharisees were doing, Jesus tells the story of the good shepherd: He says that there is a man who has a hundred sheep, but if he has lost one, he will leave the nighty-nine and go search for the lost one until he finds it.

And when the shepherd has found the lost sheep he puts it onto his shoulders and rejoices. When he comes home, he calls all friends and neighbours telling them to rejoice with him for he has found his sheep which was lost. And he rejoices more for that sheep than all the other sheep who did not go astray.

Jesus then says that whoever enters the sheep pen, not by the door, but another way is a thief or robber. But whoever enters in by the gate is the shepherd of the sheep. To him, the door opens. The sheep hear his voice, he calls his own sheep by name and leads them out. And when he puts out his sheep, he goes before them and the sheep follow him, because they know his voice. Jesus says that the sheep will not follow the voice of a stranger, but they will flee from a stranger, because they do not know the voice of a stranger.

Jesus says that He is the door of the sheep and it is only by Jesus that anyone can enter in, and they will be saved and then they can go in and out, and find pasture. Jesus said that many thieves and robbers came before him, but the sheep do not hear them. These thieves come to steal, kill and destroy, but Jesus said that He has come to provide life for everyone so that they have it more abundantly.

Jesus continued saying that He is the good shepherd, and the good shepherd gives His life for the sheep. Jesus knows his sheep, and the sheep know Him. He lays down his life for the sheep. Jesus says 'My sheep hear my voice, and I know them, and they follow me.'

Jesus says that rough Him everyone is given eternal life, and they shall never perish, neither shall any man pluck them from His hand as Our Father in heaven gave them to Jesus, He is greater than all, and so no one is able to take them from our Father's hand.

After Jesus had spoken, many did not understand what he was saying with some Jews accusing him of being possessed by demons and others reminding them of the miracles that Jesus had performed proving that He could not be possessed by demons..

This story reminds us that we are Jesus' sheep, and He is our shepherd. He leads us and guides us into green pastures, into goodness. The story shows how Jesus protects us and looks after us, so that we can trust Jesus. Jesus is the only door to enter into heaven, any other way will not get entry. We are Jesus' sheep and we will have eternal life and never perish, and no one will be able to take us from Jesus.

Jesus and the Sick Woman

(Mark 5: 25-34)

One day, Jesus was walking with His disciples surrounded by the gathering of a crowd. In the midst of the crowd a woman, who was diseased with an issue of bleeding continuously for 12 long years, came behind Jesus and reached out to touch the hem of His garment.

This woman had seen many physicians, and had spent all of her money, but nothing had healed her or made her better, instead she became worse. So when she heard that Jesus was coming, she thought within herself that if she only just touches the hem of His garment she would be made whole and healed.

Immediately after touching the hem of His garment the fountain of her blood had dried up, and she felt within her body that she had been completely healed.

Jesus knowing that someone had touched Him and His power had been manifested, He asked twice, 'who touched me?' Not so that He may gain information, because He knows all things, but so that a confession of the woman may be made to profess her faith and to glorify God.

The woman who was now fearing and trembling, knowing that she had been healed, came and fell down before Jesus. She declared to Him before all the people why she had touched Him and how she was healed immediately.

Jesus then said, 'daughter, be of good comfort; your faith has made you whole.' And the woman was immediately fully healed

This story reminds us of how powerful faith is. The woman who had this longstanding issue with bleeding had so much faith in Jesus and His power, that she believed simply touching the hem of His garment would heal her. We need to have the same faith in Jesus and His power, that by Him all things are possible. When Jesus questioned who touched Him she could have been shy and not spoken, but she was more desperate to be healed than to care about what people thought about her. Likewise we have to be more desperate for God than care what people think about us or say about us, because Jesus is who will stay for eternity, while the opinions of other people will not.

Jesus and the Girl Who Rose from the Dead

(Luke 8:40-56)

One day, Jesus returned to a crowd of people who were waiting for Him and gladly welcomed Him. A man named Jairus, ruler of the synagogue, fell down at Jesus' feet and begged desperately for Jesus to come to his house, for he had one child, a daughter who was about twelve years old, who lay dying in her bed. Jairus begged Jesus to come and lay hands on her so that she may be healed and live.

And Jesus went on His way with him, and His disciples followed, and many people also followed. As the crowd flocked Jesus, Jairus lost vision of Jesus and when he later found Jesus, there came someone from the ruler of the synagogues house, telling him that his daughter is dead and so there was no point in troubling Jesus to do anything as it was too late.

But when Jesus heard this he answered saying, "do not fear, only believe and she will be healed."

And Jesus made his way to the house of Jairus. When he got to the house, he ordered that no one must come in, except Peter, James, John and the parents of the girl.

All who were in the house wept and expressed great sadness over her, but Jesus told them, "do not weep, she is not dead but is only sleeping." They all laughed at him, knowing she is dead.

However, Jesus entered where the girl was lying and took the girl by the hand and said, "my child, get up."

Immediately her spirit returned and she got up straightaway, and walked. Jesus commanded to provide her with food. Her parents were astonished, but Jesus told them not to say what happened to anyone.

This story reminds us that we need to believe in the power of God, even if it looks impossible. With God all things are possible, that even a little girl can rise from the dead. The same power that rose Jesus from the dead lives in us, and so we need to believe and stop being so fearful when a situation looks impossible. We must learn to realise that the power of God is more powerful than any situation. We must not fear the bad situation we face, but believe in the power of God.

The Parable of the Hidden Treasure and the Pearl

(Matthew 13:44-46)

In order to get the crowds of people who followed Him to understand the great importance of obeying God's word to find favour with God and access the kingdom of heaven, Jesus told many parables to them. Jesus wanted the people to have every opportunity to be able to know about these things so that they could follow the Lord's Laws and become righteous and enter the kingdom of heaven.

One such parable was when Jesus spoke about the kingdom of heaven being like treasure that is hidden in a field. According to Jesus the treasure in the field was found by a man who was so happy that he immediately hid the treasure again and then went out and sold all that he had so that he could buy the entire field.

Similarly Jesus talked about the kingdom of heaven being like a merchant looking for fine pearls. However, as soon as the merchant found a pearl of great value, he then went away and sold everything that he had to enable him to buy that pearl.

In both parables Jesus tells, it is clear that he is saying that the kingdom of heaven is not easy to see and that those who want it must seek it. Jesus also shows that it has insurmountable value, and is priceless, so much so that when it is found, people will want to sell all their worldly possessions to have access to the eternal life that the kingdom of heaven represents.

This story shows that having access to God's eternal love when we find the kingdom of heaven will satisfy our greatest and every need but we will only find it if we are looking for it. However once found, it will satisfy all that we have ever wanted, which will ensure that we never have to search for anything else again as we will have God's true glory.

The Parable of the Mustard Seed – Gods Kingdom

(Matthew 13:31-35)

When Jesus met with the crowds He spoke in many parables to help them to understand the importance of the messages that He wanted to share about following the word of God.

For instance, when He told them about the kingdom of heaven, he likened it to a grain of mustard seed, which a man took and planted in his field.

He said that the mustard seed is the tiniest of all seeds, and because it is so small it does not look like it will produce much once it has been planted.

However, when it is grown, it is the greatest among all herbs and plants and it becomes a huge beautiful tree. The tree is so huge that many birds will fly around and choose that tree to sit on its branches and make their homes.

Jesus then told them another parable about the kingdom of heaven being like yeast. He said that a woman took some yeast and mixed it up with a large amount of flour until it had been worked all through the dough.

Jesus told the crowd that he will continue to speak in parables, saying things that no-one had heard since the beginning of creation.

This story reminds us that God will take the small and tiny things and grow them to be extremely big. It does not matter how small we may think we are, by the power of God, He will transform us into a big impact to His kingdom. Similarly, something may start small, but when we take the small and are faithful to God, it is transformed to something miraculously huge.

The Parable of the Net

(Matthew 13:47-52)

Jesus continued to tell his parables to the crowds. This time he shared with them another story about the kingdom of heaven, likening it to a net that is cast into the sea, which then gathers every kind of fish that it can capture.

However, when the net was full, the fishermen drew the net to shore. They then sat down and gathered all of the good fish into their baskets but threw all of the bad fish away.

Jesus said that this is exactly what will happen when the end of the world comes; the angels of God will come and separate all of the good people from all of the wicked people and the wicked people will be weeping and wailing as they are thrown into burning hell.

After he spoke, Jesus asked the people whether they had understood what he was trying to tell them and they said that they had.

This story reminds us what it will be like when the end of the world comes. As just as the net that was cast into the sea drew all different kinds of fish, so too does the message of the gospel that is spread into the world draw many types of people both good and bad.

However, just like the net, the good fish are kept and the bad fish are thrown away and discarded. At the end of age so too will the good Christians who follow Christ be separated from those people who bear false witness and are only masquerading as followers of Christ.

Jesus Feeds the Five Thousand

(Matthew 14: 13-21)

After the death of John the Baptist, who had been killed by King Herod, Jesus was sad and so He took a boat in order to try to find a solitary place to be alone. However the crowds heard that Jesus was leaving and had followed Him by foot from their various towns.

Once Jesus landed and saw the large crowds who had gathered, He felt compassion for them as to Jesus, they were like sheep without a shepherd. Jesus continued throughout the day teaching the people and healing the sick who came looking for Him.

Now as it had been a long day and it was getting late, the disciples came to Jesus and said, "it is now late, and we are in a desert place. Send the people away into their cities so they may eat".

But instead of sending the people away, Jesus said to the disciples, "they do not need to leave, give them something to eat". The disciples were willing but did not know how they would be able to buy and carry enough food to feed all the thousands of people that were there. Jesus told the disciples to check how much food they had with them, and there was in total: 5 loaves of bread and 2 fishes.

Jesus commanded the disciples to bring the people to him. Jesus took the five loaves and two fish, looked up into heaven, gave thanks and blessed and broke the food. He then gave out the food to His disciples to divide among all the people. And every person ate and was full. About 5000 men, as well as women and children ate from the loaves and fishes that Jesus had blessed

This story reminds us that with God all things are possible. Nothing is impossible for God. And so no matter what, God will always provide for us. When we put Him first and stay in God's presence everything else will come, without our effort but because of God's faithfulness. When we feel that we are going through an impossible situation, remember that Jesus was able to feed at least 5000 people with just 5 loaves of bread and two fishes.

Jesus Walks on Water

(Matthew 14:22-33)

One day, after preaching to the crowds Jesus tells His disciples to get into a boat and go on ahead of Him and sail across to the other side, whilst He dismisses the crowds of people that surrounded them. After the crowd had left, Jesus went off onto the mountainside to pray by himself. No matter what was going on, or how busy Jesus was, He always made time to be alone to pray to our Father in heaven.

By the time that evening came, the boat had already sailed a considerable distance from the shore, and Jesus was left alone on the land. Jesus looked up and saw that the disciples were working extremely hard in their rowing because the wind was moving against them, and pushing the waves against the boat.

As the night fell, Jesus came out to them, walking on the sea. When the disciples saw Jesus walking on the sea they thought that it was a spirit and cried out in fear because all the disciples were terrified thinking they had seen a ghost.

Immediately, Jesus talked to them and reassured them, saying, "be happy and brave, it is me, do not be afraid."
However, Peter replied, "Lord, if it is you, tell me to come to you on the water."

So Jesus told Peter to come to Him and Peter came out of the boat and began to walk on the water. However, when he saw the wind coming towards him, he became afraid and cried out for Jesus to save him. Jesus immediately reached out His hand and grabbed Peter, saying, "you have little faith. Why did you doubt me?"
As soon as Jesus climbed into the boat with Peter, the winds completely stopped and there was no longer a battle of the winds. The disciples were amazed beyond measure, and wondered at the glory of God, saying to Jesus that Truly He is the Son of God.

This story reminds us to keep our focus on Jesus always, even throughout our storms. Storms will always come to us, by bad situations or impossible situations, but the way to stay joyful throughout the storm is to keep your focus on Jesus. Peter called out for Jesus to call him onto the water and because He was focused on Jesus he didn't have any fear. But then when Peter stepped onto the water and looked around at the storm he grew afraid. That is the same as us: if we take our focus from Jesus during our storms then we will grow scared and forget about the power of our God who is right in front of us. But even when Peter grew afraid, Jesus was right there to catch him. When we grow afraid by taking our focus off Jesus, He will be right there for us. He will never let us fall.

Jesus' Transfiguration

(Matthew 9: 1-13)

One day, Jesus took His disciples Peter, John and James apart from the other disciples, and led them high up a mountain. Whilst there, Jesus was transfigured before them and His face shone as bright as the sun and His clothes became white as the light.

Suddenly there appeared before them Moses and Elias, talking with Jesus. It was a breath-taking sight! Peter asked Jesus if it was good for him and the other two disciples to be there, telling Him that if they wished He could make a shelter for each of them: one for Jesus, one for Moses and one for Elias. And while Peter spoke, a bright cloud overshadowed them.

A voice came out of the bright, bold cloud saying, "this is my beloved Son, in whom I am well pleased; listen to Him."

When the disciples heard they fell on their face in awe, and were very afraid. The disciples knew it was the voice of our Father in heaven. But Jesus came to the disciples and touched them, telling them to get up and not be afraid.

When the disciples lifted their heads they only saw Jesus, for everything else had vanished. Jesus told the disciples not to tell anyone what they had seen until after the Son of Man has been raised from the dead.

The disciples asked Jesus why the teachers of the law say that Elijah must come first. And Jesus replied, "to be sure, Elijah comes and will restore all things. But I tell you Elijah has already come and they did not recognise him, but instead they have done everything to him that they wished. In the same way, the Son of Man is going to suffer at their hands."

Then the disciples began to understand that Jesus was in fact talking to them about John the Baptist.

This story reminds us that God's word is truth. It reveals to us the beautiful power of God, and what He has and will continue to reveal to us. We will be in complete awe when we see the glory of Jesus and the kingdom of heaven, as there is nothing more beautiful and amazing.

Jesus and the Rich Young Man

(Matthew 19:16)

One day a young man came to Jesus and asked him directly, "Teacher, what good thing do I need to do to get eternal life?"

Jesus asked the young man why he had asked this question and told him that there was only one who is good, who is God almighty, however, if he wanted everlasting life then he needed to obey the commandments. The man then enquired which commandments Jesus was referring to and Jesus told him: "Do not murder. Do not commit adultery. Do not steal. Do not give false testimony. Honour your father and mother and love your neighbour as yourself."

The young man was puzzled as he stated that he has already kept to these commandments. Jesus told him that for him to be regarded as perfect, he would need to sell all his possessions and give everything to the poor and only then will he receive the treasures of heaven and can follow Jesus.

The young man was sad when he heard what Jesus told him to do because he was a wealthy man and he did not want to give up his wealth.

Jesus then said to his disciples, "I tell you the truth: it is harder for a rich man to enter the kingdom of heaven, than for a camel to go through the eye of a needle."

The disciples were shocked at what Jesus had said and asked, "who then can be saved?"

Jesus' response was, "with Man this is impossible, but with God all things are possible" Peter then reminded Jesus that they had left everything in order to follow Jesus. To which Jesus responded, "when the Son of Man sits on His glorious throne, those who have followed me will also sit on twelve thrones, judging the twelve tribes of Israel. And everyone who has left their family or fields for my sake will not only receive a hundred times as much, but they will also receive eternal life."

This story reminds us that we shouldn't love our wealth and possessions more than we love God. We must always be willing to give up our wealth for the service of God and man. In the case of the young man, he had made an idol of his wealth, and he loved it more than God. Jesus exposed the greed in the man's heart—greed the man did not even suspect he had. Jesus' statement that only God is perfect reminds us that we can only ever strive to be like God. However, if we are willing to give up everything to follow God, then we will get a hundred times more than we give up.

Jesus and the Little Children

(Mark 10:13-16)

As Jesus travelled through the different cities, all the children loved Jesus and many times ran up to Him in adoration. Many children came up to Jesus in the temple crying, "Hosanna to the son of David."

One day, several little children were brought to Jesus in the hope that He would put His hands on them and pray over them. However the disciples told them to go away, because they thought that Jesus would not want all of these little children around Him when He had so much to do.

But Jesus was not happy and told the disciples, "never forbid children to come to me; for the kingdom of heaven belongs to the children. Whoever does not receive the kingdom of God as a little child shall not enter in".

Jesus then laid His hands on the little children and departed.

This story reminds us that Jesus has time for everyone, no matter what He is doing and where He is going. The kingdom of heaven is for the children because we all have to go to God as His child. And all those who are a child of God are children when it is time to go into heaven. It does not matter how old we are, but we must act child-like to God. Not childish, but to be dependent on God, in awe of God, submissive to God, and have a soft heart, to be forgiving and loving. The same way we depended completely on our parents and not ourselves when we were young children, is the same way we must depend on God and not ourselves at all times if we are to be received into heaven.

Jesus at the Home of Martha and Mary

(Luke 10:38)

One day during Jesus and His disciple's travels, they came to a village, and a certain woman called Martha received Jesus into her home. Martha also lived with her sister Mary.

Jesus entered into the house, and sat down. Mary was completely in awe and throughout His visit she sat at His feet and listened intently to His every word.

Martha on the other hand was pretty much occupied and busy with all the preparation that she felt had to be made in honour of Jesus. However, Martha soon became quite overwhelmed with the work that she was undertaking by herself and so Martha went to Jesus and asked, "Lord do you not care that my sister has left me to do all the work on my own? Tell her to help me."

Jesus however did not tell Mary to get up and do the housework with Martha, but He told Martha that she is too troubled about many things. But Mary has chosen to be with me and learn from me which is the only thing that is needed and will never be taken away from her.

This story reminds us that nothing should come before spending time listening to the word of God, as Jesus tells us. We can often let the things of this world be our priority and then get too busy and distracted with things other than God. But Jesus is telling us that this can lead us to become irritable and heavy burdened, and that we need to focus on God. The word of God and spending time with Him is the only thing that we need and the only thing that will not be taken from us.

The Death of Lazarus

(John 11:1-16)

One day, Lazarus, who was the brother of Martha and Mary and well loved by Jesus, fell sick.

Although Mary and Martha sent word to Jesus to let Him know that their brother Lazarus whom He loved was sick, Jesus replied saying that, "this sickness will not end in death but it is so that God's Son may be glorified through it."

Jesus was not worried about Lazarus for He knew all things, and had the power to do all things. For this reason, after Jesus was told the news of Lazarus' sickness, He stayed in the place where He was for two more days.

After this He said to his disciples, "let's go into Judaea," but the disciples warned Jesus not to go there because the Jews had almost stoned Him the last time they went there.

But Jesus tells them not to worry, explaining to them that He must go to Lazarus who He says at this time had fallen asleep, but that He is going to awaken him out of sleep. The disciples replied, "if he sleeps, then he will get better." Because they thought that Jesus was talking about natural sleep but Jesus tells them that He is actually talking of Lazarus' death.

By the time Jesus and the disciples arrived in Bethany, Lazarus had been laid in his grave for four days already and many of the Jews came to Mary and Martha to comfort them for their loss of their brother Lazarus.

Martha heard that Jesus was coming and she went straight away to see him, but her sister Mary stayed at home. Straightaway Martha said to Jesus that she knows that if Jesus was there, her brother would not have died.

Jesus replied, "I know your brother shall rise again." Martha did not understand and thought He was talking about Lazarus rising again at the resurrection at the final day. But Jesus told her that, "whosoever believes in Christ, will be resurrected right now." Martha then understood and believed in Jesus, as the Son of God.

Martha went back home and called Mary discreetly, saying that Jesus the Master was coming, and is asking after Mary. Mary then got up quickly and together with other mourners rushed over to Jesus. On seeing Jesus, Mary also said to Him that Lazarus would not have died if Jesus were there.

When Jesus saw Mary and those Jews with her crying over Lazarus, He was moved in the spirit and was troubled. Jesus then asked where the grave of Lazarus was, and they led Him there and Jesus Himself wept.

Once Jesus came to the tomb, which was a cave and had a stone laid upon it. Jesus told them to remove the stone, but Martha warned Jesus saying that as it had been four days since Lazarus had been there so it will probably smell.

Jesus said, "did I not tell you that if you will believe then you will see the glory of God?"

So, they took the stone away from the cave. And Jesus spoke to our Father in heaven saying, "thank you, because you have heard me." He did not say thanks for His own sake, because He says that our Father in heaven always listens to Him, but instead it was for the sake of those around Him so that they would believe that Jesus truly is the Son of God.

Jesus then said, "Lazarus, come out."

Lazarus came forward, covered head to feet with strips of linen. Jesus said to those people standing around to help take the grave clothes off Lazarus, and let him go.

This story reminds us that Jesus was so compassionate, and even though He is our Lord and Most High, He wept for Lazarus. Jesus was such a loving, kind, gentle, warm man. And at the same time, He is Christ who is able to do all things, even bring a man back from death, showing us that all things are possible with God. Nothing is too big for our God to do. And when we believe in God, then we will see His glory.

Jesus Heals a Man Born Blind

(John 9:1-12)

One day as Jesus was walking by the road, He saw a man who was blind from his birth. Jesus' disciples asked Him, "Rabbi, who was it that sinned, this man or his parents, so that he was born blind?"

And Jesus replied saying that neither had sinned, but that his blindness was to allow the works of God to be displayed in him. For Jesus can do the works that no other man can do, because he is the Son of God.

When Jesus had spoken, he spat on the ground and made mud from it. He then anointed the eyes of the blind man with the mud. Jesus then told the blind man to go and wash in the pool of Siloam. The blind man listened, and did as Jesus had asked, washed his face, and he could see!

All of the neighbours and those who had seen the blind man begging, were confused and amazed at how he could now see. Some thought that maybe it is not the blind man, but someone who looks like him, but the healed man said, "it is me".

The man told them how Jesus had healed him, and he was brought to the Pharisees. The Pharisees made all sort of excuses, calling Jesus a sinner for healing on the Sabbath day, and did not believe he was healed, so they called the parents of the man who had received his sight.

Even though the man's parents told the Pharisees that he had always been blind, and the man who received his sight back told them again of Jesus and how he was healed saying that, "I was blind and now I see; if this man were not of God, He could do nothing." The Pharisees did not want to listen. They hurled insults at him and they threw him out.

When Jesus heard that the Pharisees had thrown the man out, Jesus found the man and asked him if he believed in the Son of Man. The man responded, "who is he Sir?"

Jesus told the man that it was He and the man said that he believed and he began to worship Jesus.

Some Pharisees heard the conversation and mocked Jesus asking if they were also blind. However, Jesus told them that if they were blind then they would not be guilty of sin, but as they can see, then their guilt remains for not believing in Him.

This story reminds us that we cannot please God without faith, and that with faith, all things are possible. Even though the man was born blind Jesus was able to heal him. We must always be faithful to God and not deny Him. The blind man did not care that the Pharisees did not believe him. He continued to say that if Jesus was not of God he could not have healed him until eventually, the Pharisees threw him out. We should continue to keep our faith, even when we are with those who do not believe in God and rebuke us.

Jesus and Zacchaeus the Tax Collector

(Luke 19:1-10)

One day as Jesus entered and passed through Jericho, there was a man named Zacchaeus, who was the chief among the tax collectors and was very rich. Although Zacchaeus wanted to see Jesus and who He was, he was not able to because the size of the crowd was so big and he was so short that he could not see past them.

So, Zacchaeus ran ahead of everyone and climbed up a sycamore tree to see Jesus, as he knew He that was going to pass that way. When Jesus came to the place where Zacchaeus was, Jesus looked up into the tree and saw Zacchaeus. However, because Jesus knows all things he called Zacchaeus by his name saying, 'Zacchaeus hurry up and come down, for today I am going to stay at your house'.

Zacchaeus speedily came down the tree and received Jesus joyfully for he was overwhelmed that Jesus wanted to stay at his house.

However when all the great crowd saw this they muttered amongst themselves, because they all saw tax collectors as one of the worst sinners, and so were very judgemental about Jesus saying that He has gone to be a guest with a man that is a sinner.

But Zacchaeus stood up and said to Jesus that he will give half of all his wealth to the poor; He also said that if he had cheated anybody out of anything or taken from someone without just cause then he will give them back four times as much as what he had taken. As Zacchaeus said all of this without being asked by Jesus. And Jesus declared that the day was a day of salvation for Zacchaeus, 'for the Son of Man came to save what was lost'.

This story reminds us that we have to be willing to give up the things we thought were important without being asked; these are things that are only important to the world, but not to God. The man Zacchaeus was so desperate to simply see Jesus and so he ran far ahead and up a tree, which is what we should be doing to encounter God. We should go out of our way, and be desperate to encounter God. Even when everyone was calling Zacchaeus a sinner, he was so willing to give up a lot of what he had without being asked, which is what showed his faith in Jesus Christ.

Jesus Clears the Temple

(Matthew 21:12-17)

By the time that Jesus entered Jerusalem, it was almost the time for the Passover celebration. People were looking for sacrifices for the tradition at the Passover meal. There was a whole group of merchants inside the Temple, selling doves, cattle and sheep for sacrifices, extremely overpriced. There were also dealers exchanging foreign money, who were sitting at tables. The people were exploiting all of those who came to visit the Temple as the Temple is supposed to be a holy place, but these people were making it into a selling ground.

Jesus enters the Temple and He was not happy at all. Jesus chased everyone out of the Temple who were engaging in these unholy activities. Jesus ran out all the cattle and sheep which were to be sold, and threw the money at the tables on the floor. Jesus threw the tables over and went to the people who were selling doves. Jesus told them to stop using God's house as a market place, and to get everything out! Jesus said, "my house will be called a house of prayer, but you are making it a 'den of robbers."

Then the blind and the lame came to Jesus and He healed them. However, because the Jewish leaders had been allowing these terrible things to take place, they were angry at Jesus embarrassing them, and although they saw the good things that Jesus had done and had heard the children shouting, "Hosanna to the Son of David".

They remained indignant, stating, "Do you hear what these children are saying?"

Jesus replied, "yes have you never read, 'from the lips of children and infants, you Lord, have called forth your praise?'"

Jesus then left the people and went and spent the night in Bethany.

This story reminds us that God is righteous and so when Jesus saw the corruption in the Temple, which was meant to be for prayer, He was rightfully angry. He fulfilled the prophecy, 'Passion for God's house will consume me'. The Temple was for all people to be able to turn to God, but those merchants and money changers were exploiting them. We must never use something, which is holy to God to exploit someone, especially if they came for God. We must not pursue selfish desire. We must pray to God that we do all things with the right intentions in our heart, and for Him to help us do so.

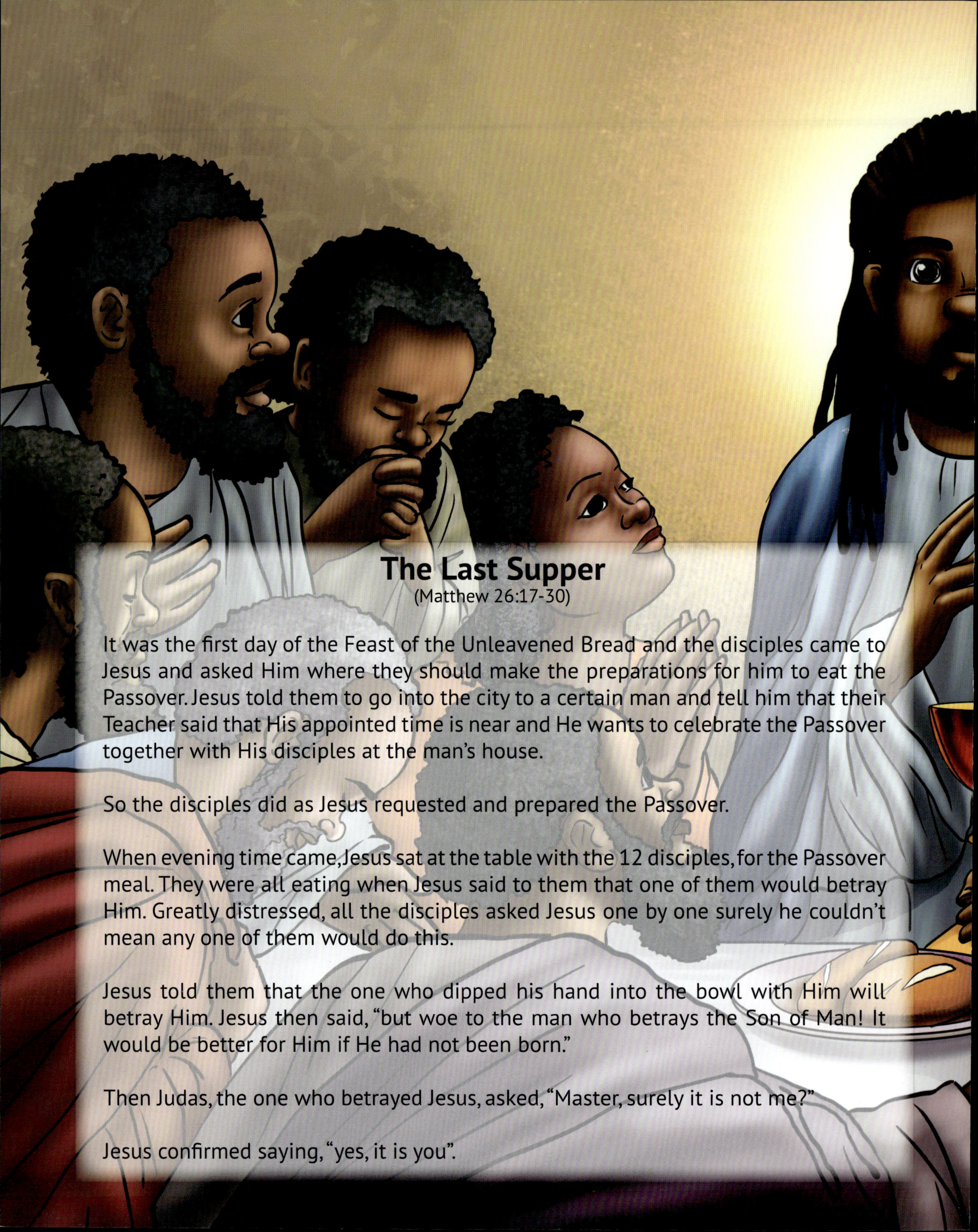

The Last Supper

(Matthew 26:17-30)

It was the first day of the Feast of the Unleavened Bread and the disciples came to Jesus and asked Him where they should make the preparations for him to eat the Passover. Jesus told them to go into the city to a certain man and tell him that their Teacher said that His appointed time is near and He wants to celebrate the Passover together with His disciples at the man's house.

So the disciples did as Jesus requested and prepared the Passover.

When evening time came, Jesus sat at the table with the 12 disciples, for the Passover meal. They were all eating when Jesus said to them that one of them would betray Him. Greatly distressed, all the disciples asked Jesus one by one surely he couldn't mean any one of them would do this.

Jesus told them that the one who dipped his hand into the bowl with Him will betray Him. Jesus then said, "but woe to the man who betrays the Son of Man! It would be better for Him if He had not been born."

Then Judas, the one who betrayed Jesus, asked, "Master, surely it is not me?"

Jesus confirmed saying, "yes, it is you".

As they were eating Jesus took some bread that was on the table, gave thanks and blessed it. Jesus then broke the bread into small pieces and gave His disciples each a piece, telling them, "take this and eat it, for this is my body."

Jesus then took a cup of wine and gave thanks to God for it, and told each of His disciples to drink from it, saying; "drink all of you, for this is my blood, which confirms the promise between God and His people. It is poured out as a sacrifice to forgive the sins of many." Jesus then said, "I tell you, I will not drink of this fruit of the vine from now until that day when I drink it anew with you in my Father's kingdom."

After they had all sung a hymn, they went out to the Mount of Olives.

This story reminds us about the Holy Communion, and the importance in what it represents. The bread, as Jesus' body, and the wine, as Jesus' blood, both of which should be taken with a pure heart. When taking the Holy Communion we should confess all our sins to God, so that we can stand right before Him, by faith in Jesus Christ, to prepare our hearts for communion. The communion is used in remembrance for the tremendous price Christ paid for our salvation, and in celebration for what we receive because of His sacrifice.

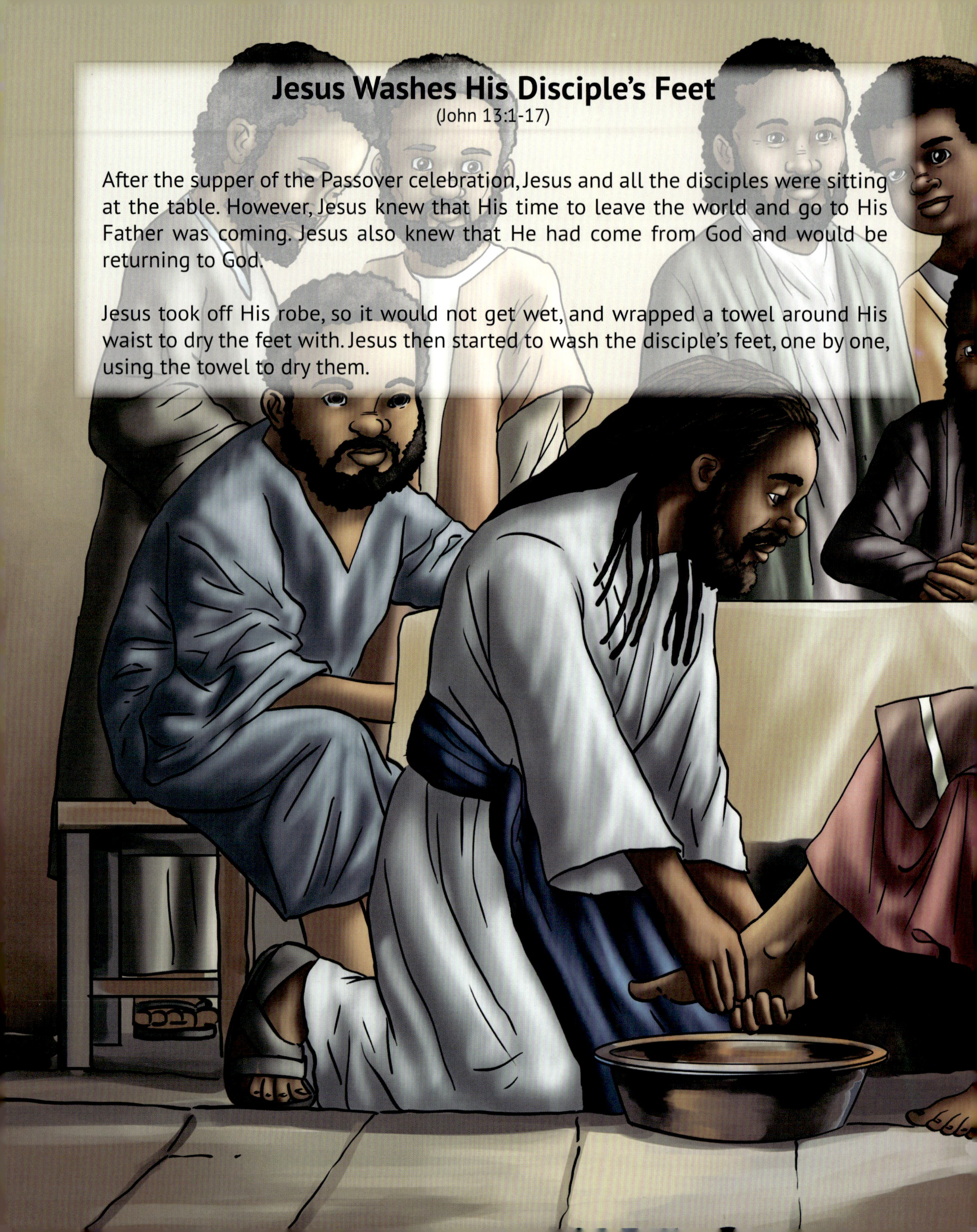

Jesus Washes His Disciple's Feet

(John 13:1-17)

After the supper of the Passover celebration, Jesus and all the disciples were sitting at the table. However, Jesus knew that His time to leave the world and go to His Father was coming. Jesus also knew that He had come from God and would be returning to God.

Jesus took off His robe, so it would not get wet, and wrapped a towel around His waist to dry the feet with. Jesus then started to wash the disciple's feet, one by one, using the towel to dry them.

When it was the turn for Jesus to wash Peter's feet, Peter asked him in shock, "are you going to wash my feet?"

Jesus then responded saying, "you won't understand now what I am doing, but later you will."

At first Peter point blank refused; He did not want His Lord washing His feet, saying, "no, you shall never wash my feet!"

Jesus simply replied, "unless I wash you, you will have no part with me." Peter then asked Jesus to not just wash his feet, but his hands and his head as well.

Jesus responds to Peter by saying a person who has had a bath, needs only his feet washed as his whole body is clean and you are clean, although not everyone of you is clean. At this point Jesus knew that He was about to be betrayed.

After washing His disciple's feet, Jesus told them that they should follow His example and wash each other's feet and they will be blessed. For He said, "no servant is greater than his Master, nor is a messenger greater than the one who sent him."

This story reminds us that Jesus, although He is King and God the Son, humbled Himself as an example to how we should live our lives, in that we should all be servants in helping each other. We must never think that we are too high up, or above someone, to be able to help, because Jesus didn't. In each step of our lives we should look for ways to help others, and ways we can better other people's lives. Using Jesus as our perfect example, we should follow Him in His perfect love.

Jesus is Arrested and Sentenced to Death

(John 18, 19)

After Jesus had finished praying with His disciples, he entered a grove of olive trees where He was approached by a huge crowd, including soldiers and temple guards all led by Judas, who knew where Jesus would be.

Because Jesus knew they were coming for Him as they approached, Jesus stepped forward, and asked who it is they were looking for. "Jesus of Nazareth", they replied. Jesus responded, "I am He", to which they all fell back and dropped to their feet. Jesus asked them again who they were looking for. And they repeated "Jesus of Nazareth."
Jesus said again, 'I told you that I am He", and then said that He will go with them, but told them to let His disciples go. All the disciples fled, except Peter and John, who followed behind separately.

They arrested Jesus, tied Him up, and took Him to Annas, the father in law to the high priest Caiaphas.

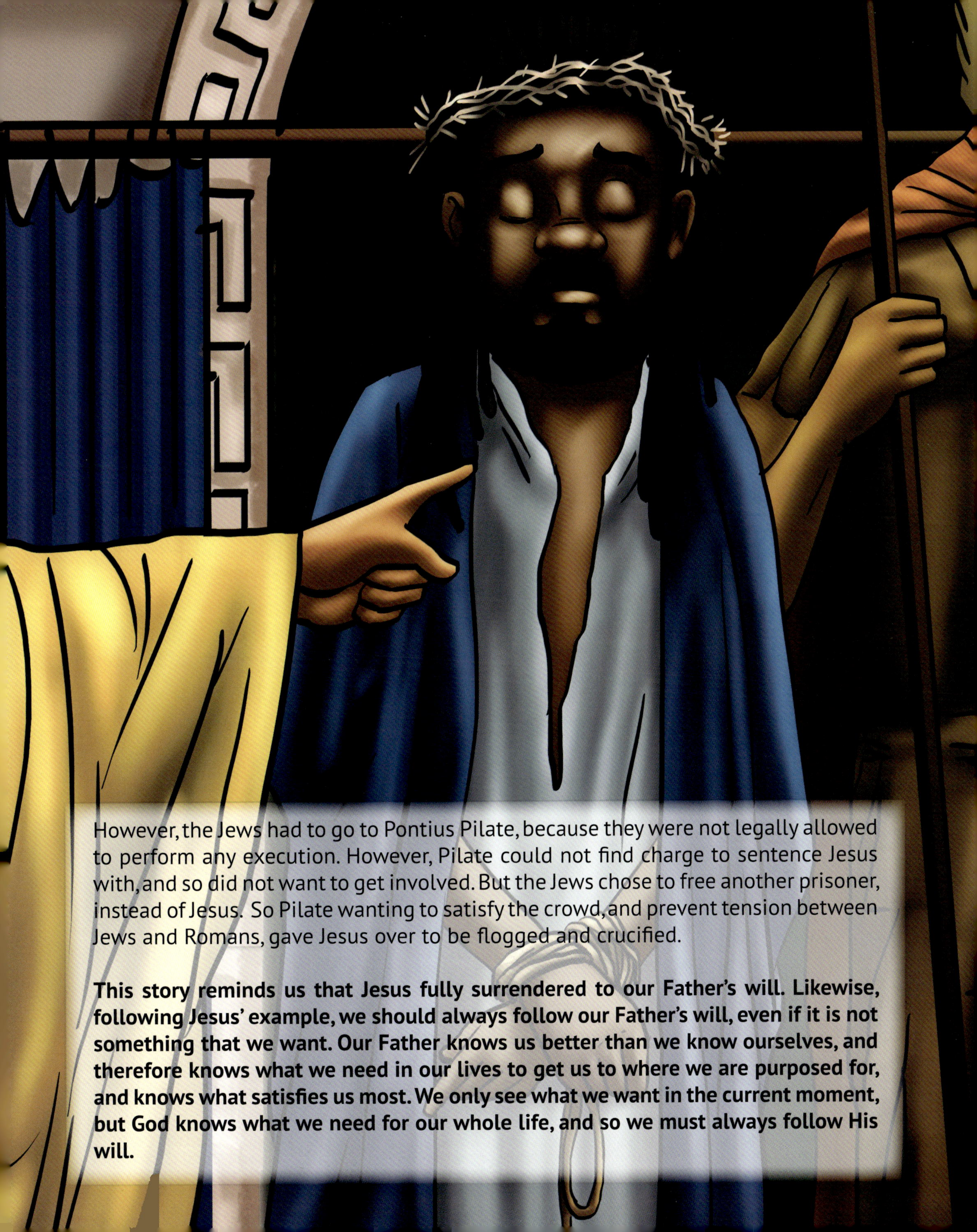

However, the Jews had to go to Pontius Pilate, because they were not legally allowed to perform any execution. However, Pilate could not find charge to sentence Jesus with, and so did not want to get involved. But the Jews chose to free another prisoner, instead of Jesus. So Pilate wanting to satisfy the crowd, and prevent tension between Jews and Romans, gave Jesus over to be flogged and crucified.

This story reminds us that Jesus fully surrendered to our Father's will. Likewise, following Jesus' example, we should always follow our Father's will, even if it is not something that we want. Our Father knows us better than we know ourselves, and therefore knows what we need in our lives to get us to where we are purposed for, and knows what satisfies us most. We only see what we want in the current moment, but God knows what we need for our whole life, and so we must always follow His will.

The Crucifixion

(John 19:17-30)

After the crowd told Pilate to crucify Jesus, Pilate said to the Jews, "here is your king," but they again told Pilate to take him away and crucify him.

The soldier took Jesus, making Him carry His own cross, which was very heavy over to the place where He was to be crucified. Two other men were led out with Jesus to be crucified, one on each side of Jesus. Jesus asked for God the Father to forgive them their sins.

The crowd and the leaders mocked Jesus. They told him to save Himself if He is really the Messiah. But Jesus needed to die on behalf of our sins, and to rise again to be able to save us. They put a sign over Jesus saying, 'This is Jesus, the King of the Jews.' But the Jews protested to Pilate saying that the sign should say that this man claimed to be the King of the Jews.

Whilst Jesus lay on the cross, the soldiers gambled for the clothes of Jesus, casting lots to see who should have it.

Jesus' mother stood near the cross, together with her sister, Mary the wife of Clopas, and Mary Magdalene. When Jesus saw his mother standing with John, one of His beloved disciples, He said to his mother, "dear woman, here is your son". Then He said to the disciple, "here is your mother," and from then on the disciple took Mary Jesus' mother into his home.

By now Jesus had become thirsty, so they soaked a sponge with some wine vinegar and put the sponge on a stalk of the hyssop plant and lifted it to Jesus' lips. Once he had received the drink, Jesus said, "it is done."

Although it was only noon and darkness fell across the whole land until three o'clock. It was so dark, as if the sun had been completely removed. Jesus then called out, "Father, Father, why have you abandoned me?"

With that Jesus bowed His head and released His spirit.

When Jesus' spirit was released, the curtain in the temple tore into two, down the middle. The earth shook, the rocks split apart and the tombs were opened.

This story reminds us that Jesus in the flesh had to experience a very painful death, and although Jesus was the Son of God, in the flesh He had the same limitation as man. Jesus called out to God the Father, asking why He had forsaken Him, because it was such a horrible death. Christ Jesus could have easily have come down from the cross to save Himself, but He chose to stay and be crucified because it was needed to be the perfect sacrifice for our sins, so that we may be reconciled to God the Father, and have the right standing with Him. The experience was also evidence of Jesus' power and status as God the Son.

This story also reminds us of how loving and caring Jesus is, as even in His last moments before death. Jesus chose not to leave Mary without someone there to physically support her, and so he told his disciple who He loved very much, to take her as his own mother. That is brotherhood, and obedience by John, as he did take her in.

Jesus Comes Alive From the Dead

(Luke 23:50-55/ 24:1-10)

After Jesus' death a good and upright man came to Pilate and asked for Jesus' body. The man then took the body, wrapped it in a linen cloth and placed it in a tomb that had been cut out of rock where no other body had been laid before.

Three days after Jesus had been crucified, Mary, Jesus' mother, and Mary Magdalene went out to visit Him at the tomb. Other female followers of Jesus also made their way to the tomb as they had prepared spices and perfumes for Jesus' body.

When the women arrived, they saw an angel sitting on the rock, which guarded the opening of the tomb, which had been rolled away from the opening.

Before the women arrived, there had been a great earthquake, where an angel of the Lord came down from heaven and rolled away the stone from the entrance and sat on it. The guards feared the angel and so they fainted. The angel's clothes were as white as snow and his face was shining like lightning.

The women were scared, and bowed their heads in fright.

The angel said to them, "why do you look for the living among the dead?" The angel then reassured them, saying, "don't be afraid! Jesus isn't here, He has risen as He said He would. Go and see for yourself. And once you see go and spread the message that He has risen to His disciples. Jesus is headed before you to Galilee, where you will see Him."

The women ran very quickly to give the message from the angel to the disciples, frightened and yet also exceedingly joyful, because of the Good News that Jesus had risen.

This story reminds us of the great power of our God, when He rolled the stone away from the entrance of the tomb. It is the point in history when they first realised that the prophesied rising of Jesus had occurred. This story also shows how everything Jesus Christ said had been true, He is an amazing God. Even when we are fearful we should obey, as the women obeyed the angel. The women were in shock and disbelief at the awesomeness of what God had done, but they were joyful, likewise to how we should be, always joyful when spreading the good news that Christ is risen indeed.

Jesus Appears to Mary Magdalene

(John 20:10-18)

After the women had found Jesus' empty tomb, Mary Magdalene had rushed to Jesus' most beloved disciples: Simon' Peter and John, whilst the other women went to the rest of the disciples.

When Simon and John heard the news, they ran to the tomb and seeing the linen wrapping that had been covering Jesus folded neatly on the floor they entered the tomb and didn't see a body. They then believed, and finally understood, what it meant in scripture that Jesus had to arise from the dead. They then went home, while Mary Magdalene stayed at the tomb.

Mary Magdalene stood outside the tomb and cried. Two angels of the Lord appeared seated in the tomb where Jesus' body had laid, one at the head and one at the foot. The angels asked Mary why she was crying. She replied that it is because she did not know where they had taken Jesus. As Mary Magdalene went to leave, she turned around and suddenly Jesus appeared, but Jesus concealed His identity so she did not realise who it was.

"Woman?" Jesus asked, "why are you crying? Who is it that you are looking for?"

However, thinking that the person she was talking to was the gardener, Mary asked him if he had taken Jesus, asking him to tell her where he had taken Jesus to so that she could go and get Him.
Then Jesus called Mary Magdalene by her name, and she at once recognised that it was Jesus. She turned to him and cried out "Teacher!", and ran to embrace Him.

Jesus told Mary Magdalene that He must to go and see the other disciples before He ascends back to heaven. Mary then ran back to the disciples and told them she had seen Jesus, and gave them His message.

This story reminds us that Jesus is very compassionate. He visited Mary Magdalene when her heart was mourning most because she thought that someone had taken Jesus, and she was dismayed she did not know where they had taken Him. But Jesus came to her and comforted her. This teaches us that God never leaves us, but is always there when we are in need of comfort.

Meeting Jesus on the Road to Emmaus

(Luke24:13-33)

After the disciples were told the message that the women at the tomb had been given by the angel, later that day two of them were travelling to a village called Emmaus. As they walked and talked, Jesus came and walked alongside them, but they did not recognise him.

Jesus asked the disciples about what they were discussing whilst they walked and they were shocked. So, one of them, Cleophas, asked Jesus if he was the only visitor to Jerusalem who had not heard about what had happened to Jesus of Nazareth.

When Jesus questioned them about what had happened, the men said that Jesus was a powerful prophet who the chief priests and rulers sentenced to death. However, when some women went to His tomb early that morning, they didn't find his body, instead they had a vision of angels who told them that Jesus had risen from the dead and was alive.

Jesus questioned them again saying how foolish they were not to believe all that the prophets had foretold about what Jesus would have to suffer before he could enter God's glory. Jesus also spoke to them earnestly about what the scriptures had predicted about His life.

As they approached the village of Emmaus, (although they still did not know that they were with Jesus), the men begged Jesus to stay with them as they said that it was getting late and Jesus agreed.

That evening as they all sat together at the table, Jesus took bread, gave thanks, broke it and began to give it to them. As He did this their eyes were immediately opened and they recognised Jesus, who then disappeared from their sight.

When the disciples realised they got up and said to each other, "were not our hearts burning when he walked and talked with us and spoke the scriptures to us?"

Then the disciples got up and returned to Jerusalem where they found the other disciples and told them that what had happened which confirmed that it was true that Jesus had indeed risen.

This story is a very important story because it reminds us of how important the scriptures from the Old Testament were in making predictions about Jesus's life, death and resurrection.

The disciples loved Jesus and they were overjoyed when he appeared to them for the first time after he had risen.

Jesus' resurrection gave the disciples so much hope. Likewise, the rising of Jesus can give us hope because it is evidence that Jesus overcame death and nothing can hold Him down. The same Spirit that rose Jesus from the dead lives in us, and so therefore we can overcome anything.

Jesus speaks to the disciples about the role of believing the prophets, and the messages passed down to all who love Him, that God will always be with us.

Jesus Appears to the Disciples and (Thomas Story)

(Luke 24:36-49, John 20:24-30)

Whilst the disciples were still marvelling about what they had been told by Cleophas, Jesus himself came and stood amongst them and said to the disciples, "peace be with you."

At this the disciples were startled and became afraid, thinking that it was a ghost who had come to be with them. But Jesus said to them, "why are you troubled? And why are you doubting that it is Me? Come and look at my hands and feet; touch and see, as a ghost does not have flesh and bones as you can see that I still have."

Although they were still unsure, they were overjoyed with amazement especially after seeing the wounds in His hands and feet. Jesus then asked them for something to eat and He then ate the piece of broiled fish that they gave Him in front of them. Jesus reminded the disciples that this is what He had told them when He was still with them; in that Everything written in the Law of Moses about Him, the Psalms and by the Prophets must be fulfilled.

Jesus then opened the minds of the disciples so that they could better understand the scriptures. He repeated what was written, that The Christ will suffer and rise from the dead on the third day and that because of this repentance, sins will be forgiven and preached in the name of Jesus. Jesus told the disciples that they are witnesses to all these things and that they will continue to preach once they have been given the power of the Holy Spirit.

One of the disciples Thomas, (who is sometimes referred to as 'doubting Thomas'), was not there when Jesus had visited the other disciples, so even though the other disciples told him that Jesus had come to them, he refused to believe that Jesus had risen and visited them, until he saw for himself and had evidence.

Thomas said, "I won't believe it unless I see the nail wounds in His hands, put my fingers into them, and place my hand into the wound in His side."

Eight days later, after Jesus had first visited the disciples, all the disciples were gathered and although the doors were locked, Jesus appeared again. This time as with the previous time Jesus again said, "peace be with you".

Jesus then spoke to Thomas directly and told him to put his fingers into Jesus' nail-pierced hands and his hand in the wound in Jesus' side. Jesus told Thomas to reach out and put his hand in His side and to stop doubting and be without faith any longer, instead he must believe!

Thomas was in such shock and humbled himself exclaiming, "my Lord and my God".

Then Jesus said to Thomas, "you believe because you have seen me. But those who believe without seeing me are blessed."

This story reminds us that our faith is not based on what we see. It is written that without faith we cannot please God. We shouldn't believe simply because we have seen, but believe even if we haven't seen, as that is the basis of faith.
Thomas felt ashamed when Jesus appeared before him, because he had such a lack of faith. We should believe because God lives within us, by the Holy Spirit, and so we do not need to see things to believe. But just as Jesus came to Thomas presenting his wounds before him, God always reveals Himself to us.
The miracles that Jesus performed throughout His life are proof that he is Christ, the son of God, to show that in believing in Him, we can have life in his name.

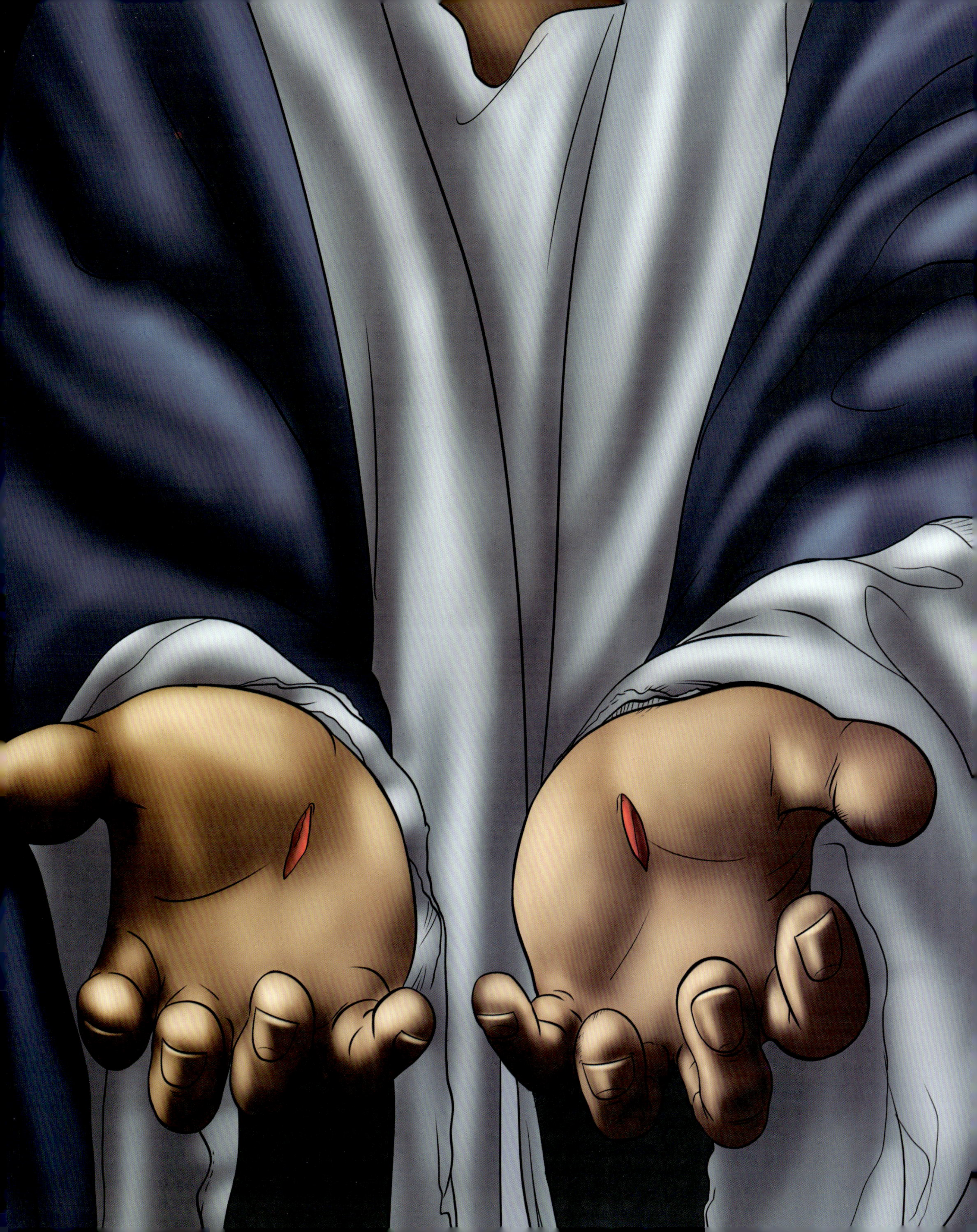

Jesus' Ascension to Heaven

(Luke 24:45-53, Acts1:10-11)

After Jesus had appeared to the disciples, following his arising from the dead, He had opened their minds so that they could better understand the scriptures and all that had been written about His life and Him rising from the dead on the third day.

It was now time for Jesus to ascend back to heaven, but He promised the disciples to send a Comforter who will always be with them, which is the Holy Spirit. The Holy Spirit is for all those who believe that they will be able to do all things, as God lives inside of them.

Jesus told the disciples to stay in the city of Galilee, after Jesus returns to heaven, until the Holy Spirit comes and fills them with power from heaven.

Jesus led the disciples to Bethany and lifted his hands to the heavens and blessed them. While Jesus was blessing them, He was lifted and taken to heaven. The disciples worshipped as Christ Jesus ascended and stared up into heaven.

Two white-robed men suddenly appeared amongst the disciples and asked them why they strained so much to see Jesus in the cloud, "Jesus has been taken from you into heaven, but someday he will return from heaven in the same way you saw him go."

The disciples then returned to Jerusalem with great joy and immediately went to the temple where they praised God continuously.

This story reminds us of God's awesomeness. When Jesus returned to heaven, He did not leave us alone, but sent the Holy Spirit, so that we will always have help in times of need. The Holy Spirit filled each disciple, and every believer should be filled with the Holy Spirit.
The Holy Spirit in you is better than having Jesus next to you because now the Spirit within us helps us to do what is right, and gives a direct connection to God.

Peter and Lame Beggar Man

(Acts 3:1-10)

There was a Levite man, lame from birth, being carried to the 'Beautiful Gate', which was the gate at the entrance of the Temple. He was carried there in order to beg for money from those people going into the temple courts.

Peter and John were on their way into the Temple, for the 3pm prayer service and the lame man was looking at John and Peter as they came close to him. As they were about to enter, the beggar asked them if they had any money. John and Peter must have looked well because they had spent so much time with Jesus, but they were not rich.

Peter and John looked at him intently, and Peter told the man, "look at us!" The lame man grew excited, thinking he was about to get a big bag of money. However, Peter said, "I do not have any silver or gold, but I will give you what I do have. In the name of Jesus, get up and walk!"

Peter took the lame man by the right hand and helped him to stand up. As he did, the ankles and feet of the lame man were instantly healed and he started to walk. The man leapt with joy and praising God, went into the Temple with John and Peter. When all the people in the temple saw the beggar, walking and praising God, they immediately recognised him as the same man who had previously begged for money at the 'Beautiful Gate' and they too were filled with awe and amazement at how the beggar man had been healed.

This story reminds us that it is so much more meaningful to provide someone with a changed life, rather than giving them a quick fix.
The lame man was looking at John and Peter to see what money they could offer him, but they had none. Peter told the man to look at him, meaning to look deep into his soul and see what he has of importance, which was God within Him, and all he could offer was his love for Jesus.

The only thing of value that we can offer people is our love for Jesus. Jesus changes people's lives. Helping the lame man with money would have been a quick fix, to perhaps bring temporary joy to his day, but Peter wanted to do more and changed his life by introducing him to Jesus, through healing him in the name of Jesus.
We need to be willing to stretch out our hands to those who need help, but we can only help those who are willing to accept our help.

Saul's Conversion

(Acts 9:1-19)

There was a man called Saul who was a Jewish rabbi who regularly made murderous threats against anyone who spoke about Jesus as their Lord. Saul's mission was to heavily persecute the church, and he travelled to Damascus to seek to get permission from the high priest to arrest any followers of Jesus that he came across on his travels and have them taken as prisoners.

During Paul's journey to Damascus, a bright light from heaven suddenly shone on him, flashing all around him. Saul fell to the ground and as he did so he heard a voice, saying, "Saul! Saul! Why are you persecuting me?"
Although Saul was startled, he asked who it was that spoke to him? And Jesus answered telling Saul that it was Jesus who spoke to him. He told Saul to get up and go to the city where he would be told what to do.

The men that had travelled with Saul were speechless because they too had seen the light and heard the voice, but could not understand it, nor see the one who was speaking. They were the witnesses, but God only revealed Himself to Saul. When Saul got up, he realised that he was blind. His companions led him to Damascus and Saul was blind for three days. He didn't eat or drink.

God spoke to a believer, Ananias, and told him about Saul and how he has been chosen by God to bring His message to the Gentiles, their kings and the people of Israel who will bear witness to Saul's suffering. So God said that Ananias must go to visit and heal Saul and God tells Saul to expect Ananias' arrival.
When Ananias arrives at Saul's house, Ananias tells Saul about Jesus, and lays hands on Saul and heals him in Jesus' name. Saul is then filled with the Holy Spirit and something similar to scales fell off his eyes, and Saul was able to see. Saul got up and was baptised.

Saul stayed in Damascus with the believers for a few days and immediately started preaching in the synagogues about Jesus. Saul changed his name to Paul, which was a name that was more common to the Gentiles, as Paul had chosen to spread the 'Good News of Jesus' to the Gentiles.

This story reminds us about the power of our God.
God transformed a man called Saul who rejected Jesus Christ and passionately hated and persecuted all believers, into the man Paul, who diligently served the Lord and spread the gospel to thousands of people, especially the Gentiles, and wrote at least 12 books of the New Testament.

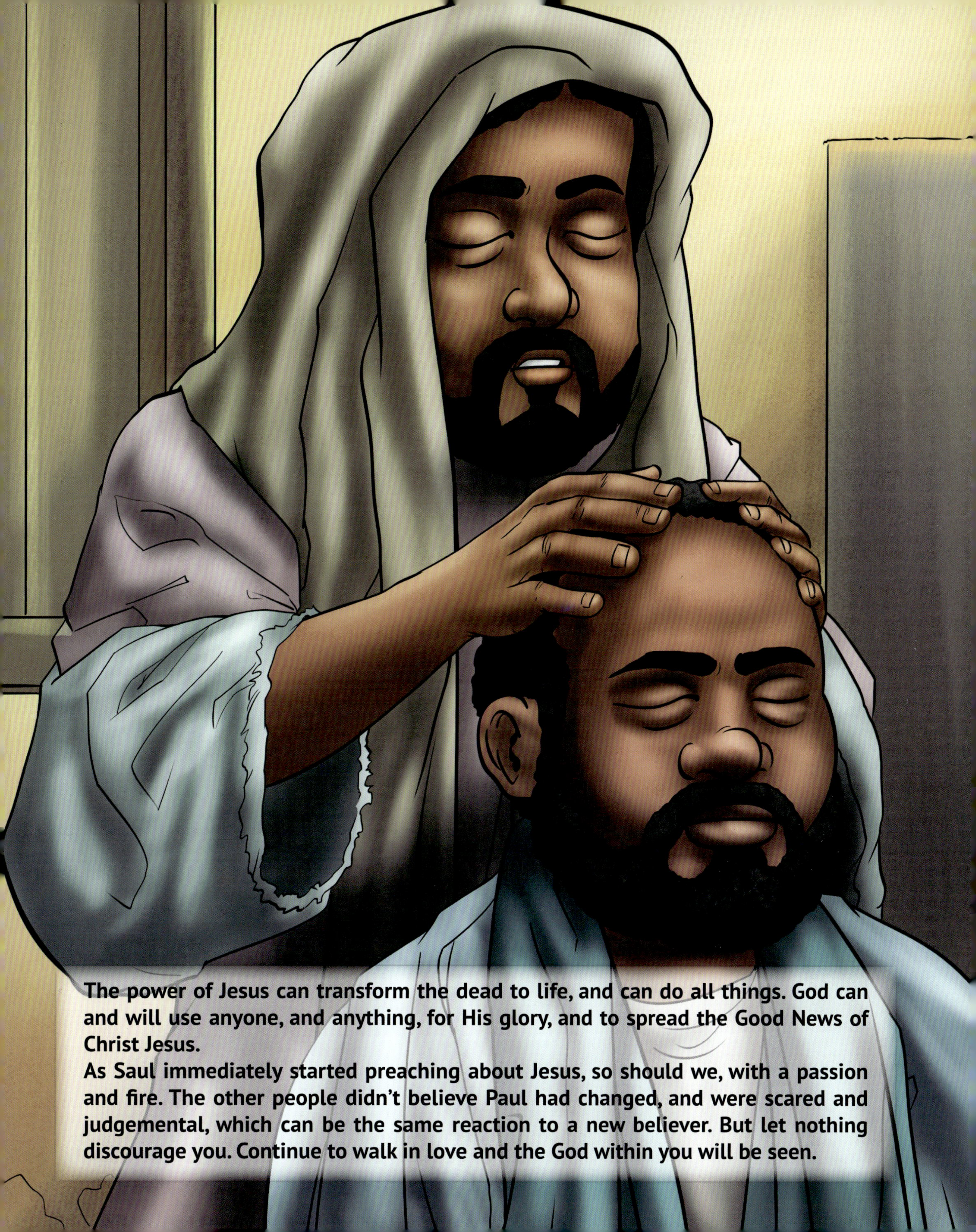

The power of Jesus can transform the dead to life, and can do all things. God can and will use anyone, and anything, for His glory, and to spread the Good News of Christ Jesus.

As Saul immediately started preaching about Jesus, so should we, with a passion and fire. The other people didn't believe Paul had changed, and were scared and judgemental, which can be the same reaction to a new believer. But let nothing discourage you. Continue to walk in love and the God within you will be seen.

Peter's Miraculous Escape from Jail

(Acts 12:1-19)

After Jesus' death, King Herod continued to try to appease the Jews by persecuting those that belonged to the church. He had already put James, the brother of John, to death and when he saw how this pleased the Jews, he decided to arrest Peter also. Peter was arrested during Passover celebration, and King Herod imprisoned him under the guard of four squads of four soldiers each. Herod's plan was to bring Peter out for public trial after the Passover, but the church was praying with deep conviction for Peter.

The night before Peter was to be on trial, he was asleep and was fastened with chains between two soldiers, while other guards stood watch at the gate. Suddenly there was a bright light and an angel of the Lord stood in front of Peter, and woke him up, telling him to quickly get up. The chains fell off Peter. The angel then told Peter to put his shoes and coat on and follow him. Which he did and followed the angel as instructed.

Peter left the cell and followed the angel, thinking the whole time that it was not real, but a vision. They passed the first and second posts that were guarded, and then they came to the iron gate that led to the city, and the gate opened for them by itself. They passed through and started walking down the road, then the angel suddenly left Peter. Peter then realised it was true and that the good Lord had sent an angel to rescue him from the clutches of King Herod and the cruel fate that the Jewish people had wanted.

Once Peter realised that he was truly free, he went to the house of Mary, the mother of John, where Mary and several other people had gathered and were praying earnestly because they knew that Peter had been arrested.

Peter knocked the door and Mary's servant Rhoda came to the door asking who it was. Rhoda was overjoyed and amazed when she recognised Peter's voice and ran back inside telling everyone that it was Peter at the door. However, no-one believed her telling her that she must be going crazy, even though Rhoda insisted that it was Peter.

Eventually, after Peter kept knocking, the door was opened and everyone saw that it was in fact Peter. Peter beckoned to them to be quiet whilst he described how he had managed to get out of prison with the help of the Lord.
Peter also told them to tell James and the brothers about what had happened and then he left them to go to somewhere safe.

The following morning, there was a huge commotion about what had happened to Peter. Herod was very angry and when he still could not find Peter after an extensive search, he ordered that all the guards be executed.

This story reminds us that God never leaves our side.
God sent angels to help Peter, and God will also send angels to help us in our hour of need. Peter was arrested because he was serving God, and spreading the Good News of Christ Jesus. We may be persecuted also, for spreading the good news about Jesus but just as we share the suffering with Jesus, we also share his glory as children of God.